Easy Macintosh®

Shelley O'Hara

que

Easy Macintosh

Easy Macintosh®
Copyright© 1992 by Que® Corporation

All rights reserved. Printed in the United States of America. No part of this book may be used or reproduced in any form or by any means, or stored in a database or retrieval system, without prior written permission of the publisher, except in the case of brief quotations embodied in critical articles and reviews. Making copies of any part of this book for any purpose other than your own personal use is a violation of United States copyright laws. For information, address Que Corporation, 11711 N. College Ave., Carmel, IN 46032.

Library of Congress Catalog Number: 91-67199

ISBN: 0-88022-819-9

This book is sold *as is*, without warranty of any kind, either express or implied, respecting the contents of this book, including but not limited to implied warranties for the book's quality, performance, merchantability, or fitness for any particular purpose. Neither Que Corporation nor its dealers or distributors shall be liable to the purchaser or any other person or entity with respect to any liability, loss, or damage caused or alleged to have been caused directly or indirectly by this book.

93 92   6 5 4 3 2 1

Interpretation of the printing code: the rightmost double-digit number is the year of the book's printing; the rightmost single-digit number, the number of the book's printing. For example, a printing code of 92-1 shows that the first printing of the book occurred in 1992.

Easy Macintosh is based on Version 6 of the Macintosh operating system.

Publisher: Lloyd J. Short

Acquisitions Manager: Rick Ranucci

Project Development Manager: Thomas Bennett

Managing Editor: Paul Boger

Book Design: Scott Cook, Karen A. Bluestein

Production Team: Scott Boucher, Sandy Grieshop, Audra Hershman, Phil Kitchel, Phil Worthington, Christine Young

Credits

Production Editor
   Cindy Morrow

Editor
   Jill D. Bond

Technical Editor
   Douglas G. White

Novice Reviewer
   Stacey Beheler

4th Dimension is a trademark of Acius, Inc.

Adobe Illustrator is a trademark of Adobe System, Inc.

Aldus PageMaker and Aldus Persuasion are registered trademarks and Aldus Freehand and SuperPaint are trademarks of Aldus Corporation.

Canvas is a trademark of Deneba Software.

CheckFree is a registered trademark of CheckFree Corporation.

Claris CAD, FileMaker, MacDraw Pro, MacPaint, and MacWrite are trademarks of Claris Corporation.

FoxBase+/Mac is a trademark of Fox Software, Inc.

Full Impact is a registered trademark of Ashton-Tate Corporation.

Heapfixer is a trademark of CE Software, Inc.

Lotus and 1-2-3 are registered trademarks of Lotus Development Corporation.

Macintosh is a registered trademark of Apple Computer, Inc.

MacTools Deluxe is a registered trademark of Central Point Software, Inc.

Managing Your Money is a registered trademark of Micro Education Corporation of America.

Microsoft Excel, Microsoft Works, and Word for the Macintosh are registered trademarks of Microsoft Corporation.

Nisus is a registered trademark of Paragon Concepts, Inc.

QuarkXpress is a registered trademark of Quark, Inc.

Quicken is a trademark of Intuit, Inc.

Ventura Publisher is a registered trademark of Ventura Software, Inc.

Wealthbuilder is a registered trademark of Reality.

Wingz is a trademark of Informix Software, Inc.

WordPerfect is a registered trademark of WordPerfect Corporation.

Trademarks of other products in this book are held by the companies producing them.

Contents at a Glance

Introduction 1

The Basics 13

Task/Review 33

Reference 181

Index 195

Contents

Introduction 1
- Why You Need This Book 5
- How This Book Is Organized 5
- How To Use This Book 6
- How To Follow an Exercise 10
- Where To Get More Help 10

The Basics 13
- Understanding Your Computer System 14
  - Hardware 15
  - More on Floppy Disks 16
  - More on Hard Disks 17
  - System Software 17
- Using a Mouse 18
- Using Your Keyboard 19
- Understanding the Desktop 22
  - Files, Folders, and Icons 22
  - Standard Desktop Items 24
- Selecting a Menu Command 25
- Working with Windows 27
- Taking Care of the Macintosh 28
- Understanding Key Terms 30

Task/Review 33
- Alphabetical Listing of Tasks 34
- Working with Disks and Windows 37
  - Start the Macintosh 38
  - Shut down the Macintosh 40
  - Restart the Macintosh 42
  - Open a disk icon 44
  - Close a window 46

v

Contents

    Move a window 48

    Resize a window 50

    Zoom a window 52

    Insert a disk 54

    Initialize a disk 56

    Eject a disk 58

    Rename a disk icon 60

    Display information about a disk 62

    Erase a disk 64

    Copy the contents of a floppy disk to a hard disk 66

    Copy a floppy disk to another floppy disk 68

Viewing the Desktop 71

    Move an icon 72

    Arrange icons 74

    Open a folder 76

    Select a window 78

    Scroll a window 80

    View a window by small icon 82

    View a window by name 84

    View a window by date 86

    View a window by size 88

    View a window by kind 90

Working with Folders 93

    Create a new folder 94

    Rename a folder 96

    Display information about a folder 98

    Copy a folder 100

    Delete a folder 102

    Retrieve an item from the Trash 104

    Empty the Trash 106

Easy Macintosh

Contents

Working with Documents and Applications............109
- Display information about a document............110
- Lock a document................112
- Duplicate a document................114
- Rename a document 116
- Move a document to another folder................118
- Copy a document to another folder 120
- Copy a document to another disk 122
- Delete a document................124
- Find a document................126

Working with Accessories 129
- Change the Desktop pattern................130
- Change the speaker volume................132
- Change the date 134
- Change the time 136
- Change the alert sound 138
- Display the time 140
- Set an alarm 142
- Use the calculator 144
- Display a special character................146

Working with HyperCard Stacks 149
- Open the Addresses With Audio stack................150
- Quit HyperCard 152
- Add a new address card................154
- Display a different address card 156
- Find an address card................158
- Add a note to an address card 160
- Edit an address card 162
- Delete an address card 164
- Open the Appointments With Audio stack........166
- Display a different appointment date................168

vii

Contents

    Add an appointment 170
    Find an appointment card 172
    Add a note to an appointment card 174
    Edit an appointment card 176
    Delete an appointment 178

Reference 181

    Quick Reference Guide 182
    Software Guide 183
        Types of Applications 183
        Word Processors 184
        Spreadsheets 185
        Databases 186
        Graphics 187
        Desktop Publishing 187
        Communication 188
        Integrated Programs 189
        Financial Programs 189
        Education 190
        Games 190
        Desk Accessories and Utilities 190
        Others 191
    Glossary 191

Index 195

Introduction

Easy Macintosh

Introduction

Congratulations. You have at your disposal one of the best tools ever created—the Macintosh computer.

What can you do with a Macintosh? Everything that you can do with any other personal computer. What does that mean? Well...everything.

With the Macintosh, you can type professional-looking letters, draw a map to your house, create letterhead, balance your checkbook, pay your bills electronically, create charts, inquire about stock prices, play games, do homework, learn how to type, and so on, and so on.

To accomplish anything on the Macintosh, however, you need a program or application. (The terms *program*, *application*, and *software* are used interchangeably. Sometimes the terms are combined: application program, software application—they mean the same thing.)

Think of a program as a specialist hired to perform a task. You might need an accountant to calculate your budget and taxes, a typist to do mailings, an artist to create a logo, a stockbroker to quote stock prices, and so on. Rather than have a specialist, you have a program. For accounting tasks, you might use a spreadsheet program. For typing letters, you would use a word processor. You can use a drawing program for creating maps and logos. Each of these programs runs on the Macintosh.

The Macintosh and programs go hand-in-hand. You can do some things with the Macintosh by itself, but you cannot do anything with applications unless you have a Macintosh.

The programs are designed to perform specific functions, and the Macintosh is designed to perform other functions. In particular, the Macintosh is used to

Start programs. You store your programs on the Macintosh. To start and use the program, you first start the Macintosh.

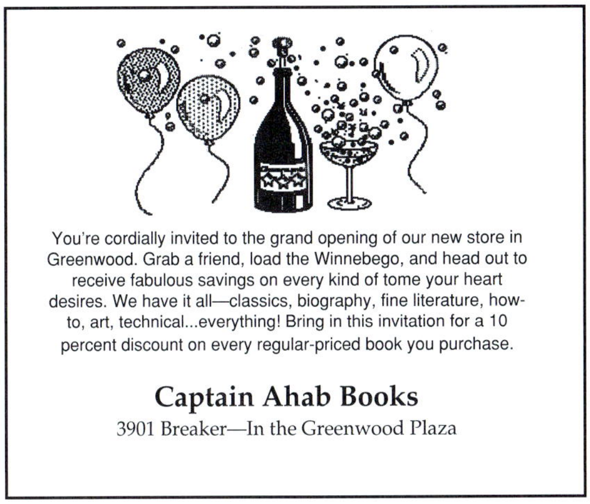

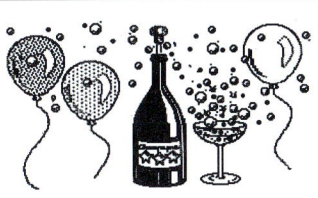

You're cordially invited to the grand opening of our new store in Greenwood. Grab a friend, load the Winnebego, and head out to receive fabulous savings on every kind of tome your heart desires. We have it all—classics, biography, fine literature, how-to, art, technical...everything! Bring in this invitation for a 10 percent discount on every regular-priced book you purchase.

Captain Ahab Books

3901 Breaker—In the Greenwood Plaza

Patricia W. Sexton
56C Rochester Rd.
Indianapolis, IN 46032
(317) 555-3491

The Pat Sexton Data Sheet

1992

P.W. Sexton

Field experience backs claims

- **Documentation Consultant**
  Leiber, Johnson and Company, Indianapolis, Indiana.
  Responsible for writing and editing documents for the software consulting and development group.
  Designed, wrote and edited user manuals, training materials, client newsletters and promotional pieces. Worked cooperatively with software designers and programmers. Wrote grammar and style guidelines used by over 100 employees in four offices.
  August 1989 to present.
- **Editor**
  Reflections Yearbook, Clarkston University.
  Supervised and delegated responsibilities to publications staff of 15. Edited and wrote copy. Organized, designed and implemented book format. Integrated a word processing and automatic indexing system into the office. Received numerous awards including the Indiana Collegiate Press Association's Book of the Year award.
  September 1987 to June 1989
- **Staff Writer**
  Clarkston Herald, Clarkston University.
  Efficiently met weekly deadlines to produce quality reviews for the university newspaper. Doubled the paper's burgeoning entertainment section. Awarded honors for Best Review by the Indiana Collegiate Press Association.
  January to May 1988. ❑

Bright, ambitious and creative writer seeks public relations position

A writer, an editor, a designer, Pat Sexton has spent the last five years perfecting her craft. She now wants to apply her talents and experience to a public relations job where she can create copy for promotional pieces.

While an English major at Clarkston University in Clarkston, Ind., Pat edited the yearbook and wrote for the school paper. She won various regional awards for both positions, including Book of the Year from the Indiana Collegiate Press Association.

After graduation, Pat turned her attention toward technical writing. She has worked since August, 1989 at Leiber, Johnson and Company, the nation's fifth largest certified public accounting and consulting firm.

Pat wears many different hats at her current position. The newsletter editor for the software development team, she also writes technical manuals, training courses and promotional materials. Her internal Style Guide is used by over 125 Leiber, Johnson employees in five offices throughout the midwest.

In her spare time, Pat serves as chapter newsletter editor for the Society for Technical Publications.

A bright, ambitious worker, Pat is ready to apply her solid writing and editing skills and step into the fast-paced world of public relations. ❑

The Sexton Education File

BA Clarkston University
Clarkston, Indiana
June, 1989
Major English
Minor Psychology

Memberships
- Member, Sigma Delta Delta, International English Honor Society
- Member & Newsletter Editor, Society for Technical Publications

Manage documents. An application creates a document. For example, a letter, a budget, and a mailing list are all separate documents. (Sometimes the words *file* and *document* are used interchangeably. Both terms mean the same thing.) You can use the Macintosh to display documents, copy documents, move documents, rename documents, and perform other file-management tasks.

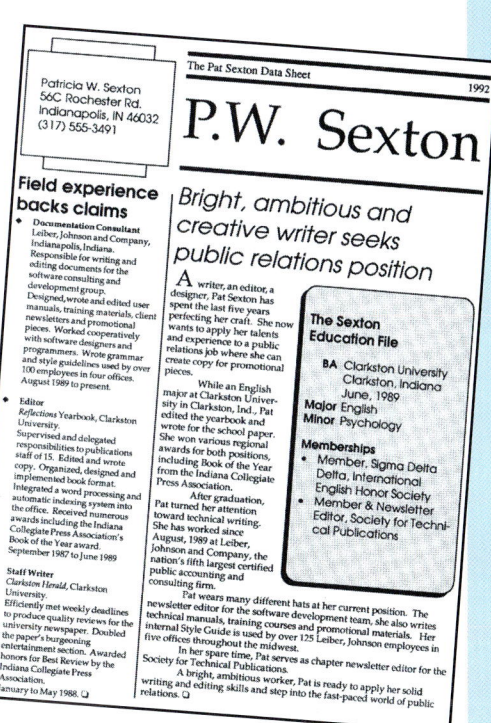

MEMORANDUM

TO: All Employees
FROM: Melissa Lowery
DATE: December 29, 1991
RE: New In-House Illustrator

I am pleased to announce that Susan Trautman has recently joined our staff as an in-house illustrator.

For the past two years, Susan has been working as a free-lance illustrator, and her outstanding drawings have enhanced several of our best-selling children's books. Most recently, Susan's work has graced *Peter Goes to the Salad Bar* and *Zachary Meets the Baby Sitter*.

Susan's experience includes over a decade of illustration and layout experience in both the publishing and advertising fields. We are all excited about the possibilities opened to us by bringing Ms. Trautman on our staff full-time.

Please join me in welcoming Susan to the McBryer Publishing staff.

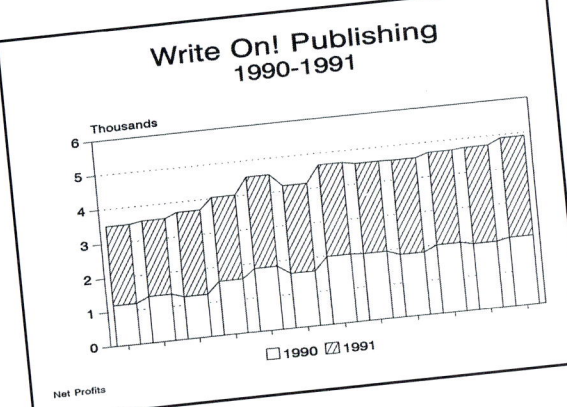

Use Macintosh desk accessories. A desk accessory (also called a DA) is a miniprogram with a limited function (display the time, calculate numbers, hold notes, and so on). The Macintosh comes with several desk accessories, including an alarm clock, calculator, notepad, and puzzle.

Learn new programs. All Macintosh programs follow the same basic guidelines; many use similar menus and commands. These programs work essentially the same way. After you learn one Macintosh program, you can easily learn other Macintosh programs.

Why You Need This Book

This book is designed to make learning to use the Macintosh *easy*. This book helps the beginning Macintosh user perform basic operations. You don't need to worry that your knowledge of the Macintosh is limited. This book teaches you all you need to know for basic operations.

You don't need to worry that you might do something wrong and ruin a program or the Macintosh. This book points out mistakes you might make and shows you how to avoid them. This book explains what to do when you change your mind—how to escape from a situation.

Reading this book will build your confidence. It will show you what tasks are necessary to get a particular job done.

Remember: The Macintosh does only what you tell it to do. Don't tell it to delete a document unless you would do the same thing manually (that is, send the only remaining copy of that document through a shredder).

How This Book Is Organized

This book is designed with you, the beginner, in mind. The book is divided into several parts:

- Introduction
- The Basics
- Task/Review
- Reference

This Introduction explains how the book is set up and how to use the book.

The next part, The Basics, outlines general information about your computer and its keyboard layout. This part explains basic concepts, such as using the mouse, selecting commands, and understanding the Macintosh display.

The main part of the book, Task/Review, tells you how to perform a particular task. The first task explains how to start the Macintosh.

The last part, Reference, contains a quick reference for performing common Macintosh operations, a software guide of different Macintosh programs, and a glossary of common computer and Macintosh terms.

How To Use This Book

This book is set up so that you can use it several different ways:

- You can read the book from start to finish, or you can start reading at any point in the book.
- You can experiment with one exercise, many exercises, or all exercises.
- You can look up specific tasks you want to accomplish, such as moving a window.
- You can flip through the book, looking at the Before and After screens, to find specific tasks.
- You can read just the Task, just the Review, or both the Task and Review sections. As you learn the program, you might want to follow along with the exercises. After you learn the program, you can use the Review section to remind yourself how to perform a certain task.

- You can read any part of the exercises you want. You can read all the text to see both the steps to follow and the explanation of the steps. You can read just the text in red to see the actions to perform. You can read just the explanation to understand what happens during a particular step.

As you read, you don't have to worry about making a mistake. All tasks have an Oops! note that explains how to get out of a situation. The book also points out errors you might make.

Task section

The Task section includes numbered steps that tell you how to accomplish certain tasks, such as copying a document. The numbered steps walk you through a specific example so that you can learn the task by doing it. Blue text below the numbered steps further explains the concept.

Oops! notes

You might find that you performed a task, such as deleting a file, that you did not want after all. The Oops! notes tell you how to undo each procedure or get out of a situation. By showing you how to reverse nearly every procedure, these notes enable you to use your Macintosh more confidently.

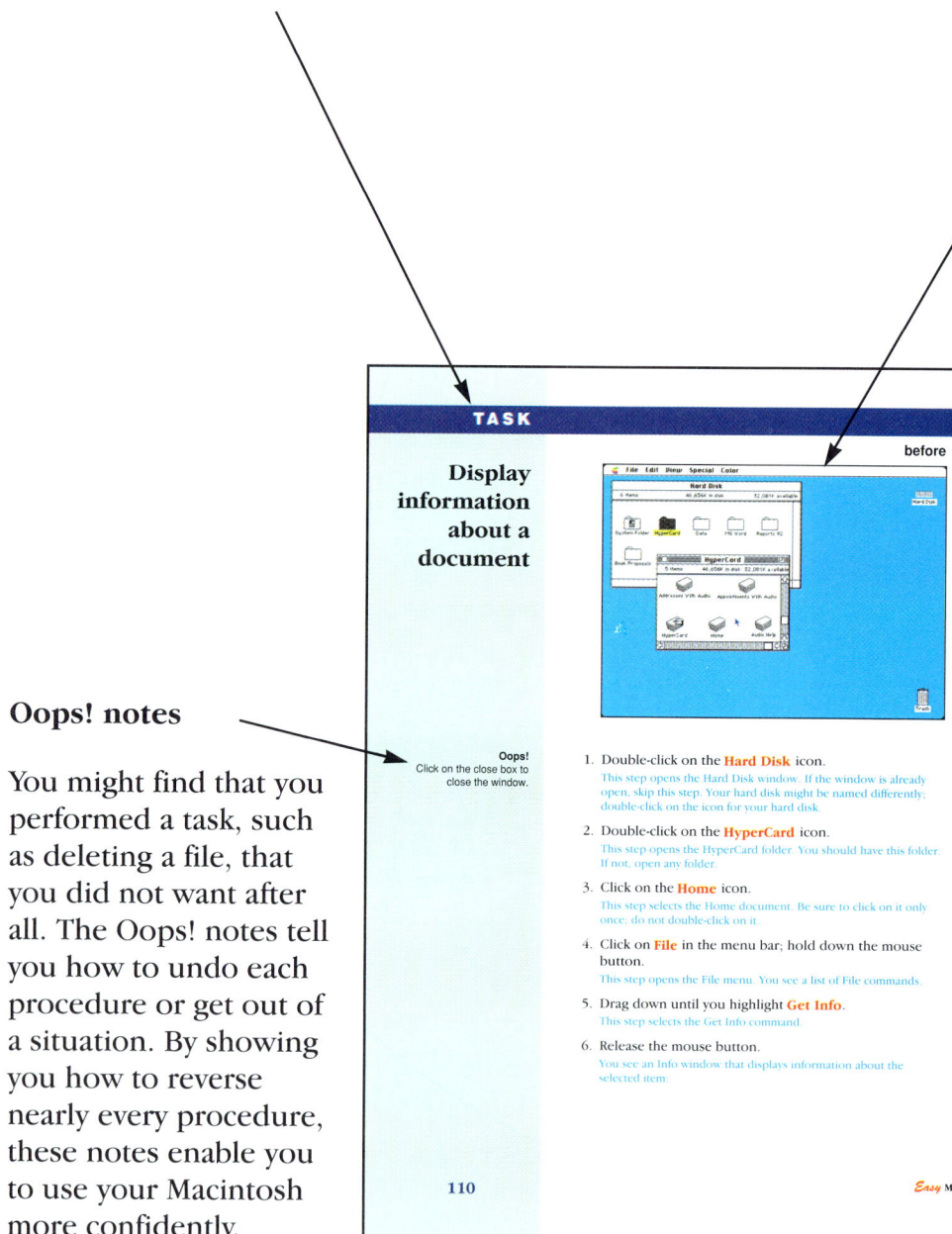

Before and After Screens

Each task includes Before and After screens that show how the computer screen will look before and after you follow the numbered steps in the Task section.

Other notes

Each task contains other short notes that tell you a little more about the procedure. These notes define terms, explain other options, refer you to related sections in the book, and so on.

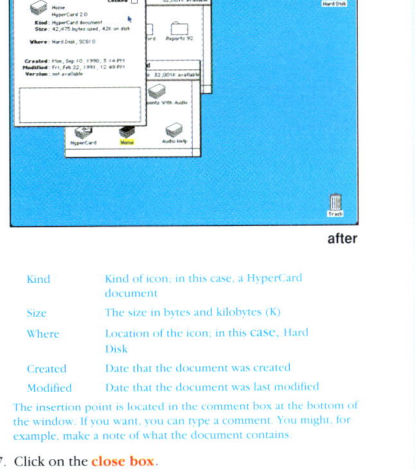

Try a shortcut
Select the document and press the ⌘-I keyboard shortcut to select the Get Info command.

Review section

After you learn a procedure by following a specific example, you can refer to the Review section for a quick summary of the task. The Review section provides more general steps for completing a task so that you can apply those steps to your own work. You can use these steps as a quick reference to refresh your memory about how to perform procedures.

To display information about a document

Introduction

How To Follow an Exercise

The Macintosh is flexible because it enables you to perform a task many different ways. For consistency, this book makes certain assumptions about how your computer is set up and how you use a Macintosh. As you follow each exercise, keep the following key points in mind:

- This book assumes that you have a hard drive and that you have already set up your Macintosh and installed the System and Finder software. (See the Basics section for a definition of these two items.)

- This book shows the screens in color, but you might not have a color monitor. If your monitor is monochrome (see the Basics part for details), or if you use different color settings, your screens will appear differently.

- Only the Before and After screens are illustrated. Screens are not shown for every step within an exercise. Where necessary, the text discusses screen messages and how to respond to them.

- You might see the windows displayed in the Before and After screens in a different location or different size than on your screen. You can arrange the appearance of the screen, and the Macintosh remembers how the screen looked the last time you used it. Also, your screen might contain different icons, folders, and documents than the Before and After screens. These differences simply mean that you have different programs, files, and folders on your Macintosh.

Where To Get More Help

This book does not cover all Macintosh features or all ways of completing a task. This book is geared toward the beginning user—someone who wants just the basics. This user isn't ready for advanced features, such as running more than one program or customizing the Desktop.

As you become more comfortable, you might need a more complete reference book. Que offers several Macintosh books to suit your needs:

The Big Mac Book, 2nd Edition

The Little Mac Book, 2nd Edition

The Mac Classic Book

Using the Macintosh with System 7

Que also offers several books on specific Macintosh programs:

HyperCard 2 QuickStart

PageMaker 4 Quick Reference

QuarkXPress 3.1 Quick Reference

System 7 Quick Reference

Using Excel 3 for the Macintosh

Using FileMaker Pro

Using MacDraw

Using PageMaker: Macintosh Version, 2nd Edition

Using Word 5 for the Mac, Special Edition

Also of interest:

Introduction to Personal Computers, 2nd Edition

Que's Computer User's Dictionary, 2nd Edition

The Basics

Understanding Your Computer System

Using a Mouse

Using Your Keyboard

Understanding the Desktop

Selecting a Menu Command

Working with Windows

Taking Care of the Macintosh

Understanding Key Terms

Easy Macintosh

The Basics

Understanding Your Computer System

When you talk about the Macintosh, you can be talking about both the hardware and the software. The *hardware* is the physical components of the Macintosh (such as the mouse, the keyboard, and the screen). The *software*—in this case, the System software—is what communicates with the hardware. The System software tells the Macintosh when to display an item on-screen, when to print a document, or when to issue a command.

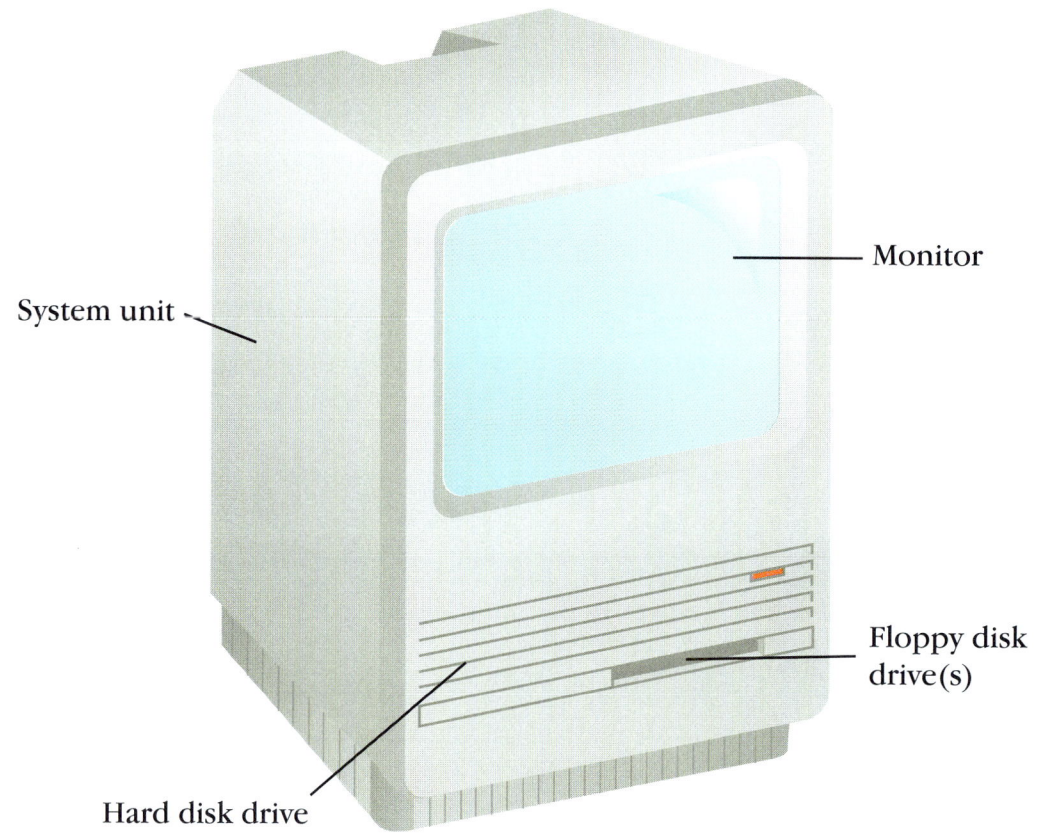

Monitor

System unit

Floppy disk drive(s)

Hard disk drive

Easy Macintosh

Hardware

Your computer system is made up of these basic parts:

- The system unit
- The monitor
- The keyboard
- The floppy disk drive(s)
- The hard disk drive
- The mouse

You also might have a printer and a microphone.

System unit. The system unit is the box that holds all the electrical components of your computer. The floppy disk drive and hard disk drive also are usually inside the system unit. (The size of the system unit varies.) The power switch usually is located on the back of the system unit.

Monitor. The monitor displays on-screen what you type on the keyboard. Your monitor and system unit might be all-in-one or separate items. Your monitor might also have a power switch. If so, be sure to turn on the monitor, also.

Keyboard. The keyboard enables you to communicate with the computer. You use it to type entries and to issue commands. You type on the keyboard just as you do on a regular typewriter. A keyboard also has special keys that you use. (Different computers have different keyboards.) These keys are discussed in the section *Using Your Keyboard*.

Floppy disk drive. The floppy disk drive is the door into your computer. It allows you to put information on the computer—onto the hard drive—and to take information off the computer—onto a floppy disk.

Hard disk drive. The hard disk drive stores the programs and files with which you work.

Mouse. A mouse is a pointing device that enables you to point to what you want on-screen, select windows, and issue commands.

Printer. A printer gives you a paper copy of your on-screen work. To print, you need to attach and install a printer.

More on Floppy Disks

All *floppy disks* basically look the same; they are 3 1/2 inches in size and are encased in hard plastic. (The floppy part is the magnetic disk inside.) Disks differ in the amount of information they can store. The amount of information is measured in kilobytes (abbreviated K). One kilobyte equals around 1000 bytes (1024 to be exact), and one byte equals about one typed character.

Very old Macintoshes used single-sided disks that were capable of storing only about 400,000 characters of information (or 400K). These disks are now generally obsolete.

The standard Macintosh disk is double-sided (meaning that it can store information on both sides of the disk, much like a phonograph record). This disk is capable of storing around 800,000 characters of information (or 800K). This disk is called double-sided double-density (sometimes abbreviated DSDD).

A newer disk is the double-sided high-density disk (DSHD). This disk can store 1.44 megabytes of information. (A megabyte is 1024 kilobytes and is abbreviated M or meg.) The drives that can use these disks are sometimes called SuperDrives or high density drives.

The disk type you use must match your disk drive. If you have a drive that can read only 800K disks, you can use only 800K and 400K disks. If you have a drive that can read 1.44M disks, you can use either 800K or 1.44M disks.

Floppy disks are usually blank when you purchase them (some companies have begun selling preformatted disks). To prepare a disk for use, you must initialize (format) it. See *TASK: Initialize a disk* in the Task/Review part.

More on Hard Disks

A hard disk is similar to a floppy disk in that it stores information, but a hard disk is much larger and much faster. Small hard disks can contain as much as 25 times the data stored on a floppy disk. Hard disks are measured in megabytes (M or meg) and come in various sizes: 20M, 40M, 80M, 100M, and up.

A hard disk is also hard (rather than floppy) and is usually encased in the system unit. (You can add an external hard drive—a drive that is a separate drive outside the system unit.) Some programs require a hard disk. This book assumes that you have a hard disk.

System Software

The Macintosh System software consists of two parts: the System software and the Finder. The System is the basic program the Macintosh uses to start itself (sometimes called *booting*). Without the System, you cannot start or use the Macintosh.

The Finder creates the Desktop (the Macintosh screen) and enables you to display and manage files. The Finder and the System are stored in the System Folder and together are known as the Macintosh operating system.

Note: The newest System software is System 7. This book is based on System 6. If you have System 7, most features work the same way. If you are using System 7, you might consider purchasing a System 7 book (such as Que's *Using the Macintosh with System 7*) when you become more comfortable with Macintosh basics.

Using a Mouse

The *mouse* is a pointing device. When you move the mouse on your desk, the mouse pointer moves on-screen. You can use the mouse to tell the Macintosh what to do; for example, you can tell the Macintosh to

- Open windows
- Close windows
- Open menus
- Select menu commands
- Select text
- Drag an item to the Trash
- Eject a disk

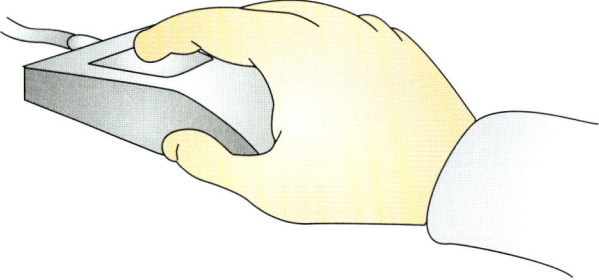

Using the mouse is the easiest and most natural way to learn any program. For some tasks, however, using the keyboard is easier. You cannot, for example, type with the mouse. In most programs, you use both the mouse and the keyboard.

There are several basic types of mouse actions, including:

Action	Procedure
Point	Position the mouse pointer on an item. Be sure to place the tip of the mouse pointer on the item.
Click	Point to an item, and then quickly press and release the mouse button.
Double-click	Point to an item and press the mouse button twice in rapid succession.
Drag	Point to an item. Press and hold down the mouse button, and move the mouse. When the item is at the desired location, release the mouse button.

Keep these terms in mind as you follow a task.

If you double-click the mouse and nothing happens, you might not have clicked quickly enough, or the pointer might not be in the right place. Make sure that the tip of the pointer is where you want it and try again.

Using Your Keyboard

In addition to using the mouse to tell the Macintosh what to do, you also can use the keyboard. A computer keyboard is just like a typewriter, only a keyboard has additional keys:

- Numeric keypad keys
- Arrow keys
- Other special keys, such as Option and Command

Depending on the type of Macintosh you have, your keyboard might look different. You can familiarize yourself with the keyboard by reading the names on the keys.

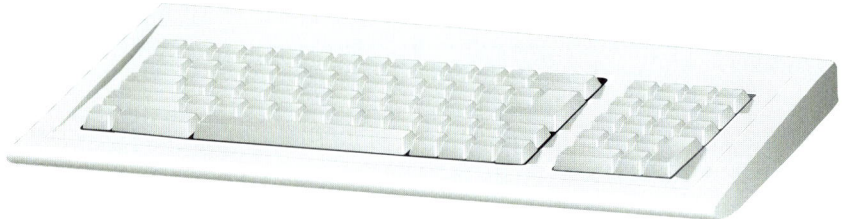

Macintosh Plus Keyboard

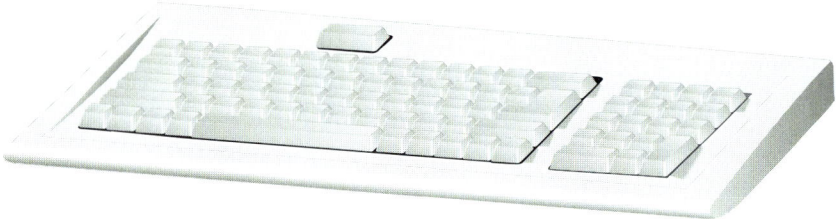

Macintosh SE Keyboard

Macintosh Extended Keyboard

Different keys perform different actions, depending on the program you are using. In general, the keys perform these actions:

Numeric Keypad. The numeric keypad enables you to enter numbers quickly (as if you were working with a calculator). The keypad contains keys for performing common math calculations, such as multiplication (*) and division(/). The Enter key confirms your numeric entry. The Clear key clears (deletes) a numeric entry. Different application programs might respond differently.

Arrow keys. The arrow keys let you move around on-screen or select text when you are using a program.

Shift. The Shift key on your Macintosh functions similarly to the Shift key on a typewriter. Pressing this key makes text uppercase and selects different special characters.

Ctrl (*Control key*). The Ctrl key serves different purposes, depending on the program that you are using.

Option. The Option key accesses special characters such as ™ and ®. This key has various functions, depending on the application program you are using.

Command (or ⌘). The Command key accesses menu commands quickly. Pressing the ⌘-N keyboard shortcut, for example, selects the New Folder command.

Return. The Return key confirms a command or inserts a carriage return when typing.

Delete. The Delete key deletes characters to the left of the insertion point.

This book indicates key combinations (also called *keyboard shortcuts*) with a hyphen. To use a keyboard shortcut, hold down the first key. While holding down the first key, press the second key. Then release both keys. If you were to use the ⌘- N keyboard shortcut, for example, you would press and hold down the ⌘ key, type the letter N, and then release both keys.

Understanding the Desktop

When you first turn on the Macintosh, you see the Desktop. (If you want to follow along, turn on your Macintosh. See *TASK: Start the Macintosh* in the Task/Review part.) The computer Desktop is similar to your desk or office.

Files, Folders, and Icons

Think about how you store items in your office. In your office, you might have a filing cabinet. In that filing cabinet, you probably have folders that pertain to different projects, clients, patients, or some other grouping—maybe logical, maybe not. Within each folder you have articles, letters, diagrams, reports—anything you want to save. This storage method carries over to the Macintosh.

On the Macintosh, the hard disk is your filing cabinet. On that disk you have *folders*, and within a folder you have *files* (individual documents). The same items that you store in a paper folder (memos, articles, diagrams) are stored in electronic form in a file on the Macintosh.

Items that appear on the Desktop are represented by pictures, which are called *icons*. Folders are represented by icons that look like folders. In most cases, files are represented by icons that look like documents. Applications are also represented by icons. These are folder icons:

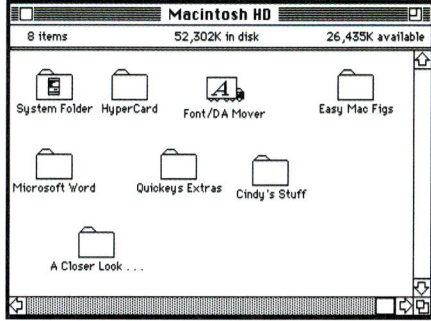

These are file icons:

These are icons for specific applications (HyperCard, Microsoft Word, and QuickKeys):

The Basics

Be sure to use some method of organizing files. You might organize by project or by client or by application. Pick one method and stick to it. The following illustration shows several ways to organize files:

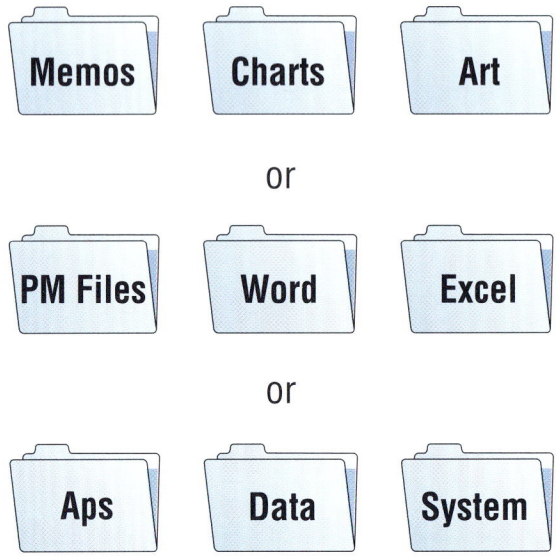

Keep in mind that you can store folders within folders.

Standard Desktop Items

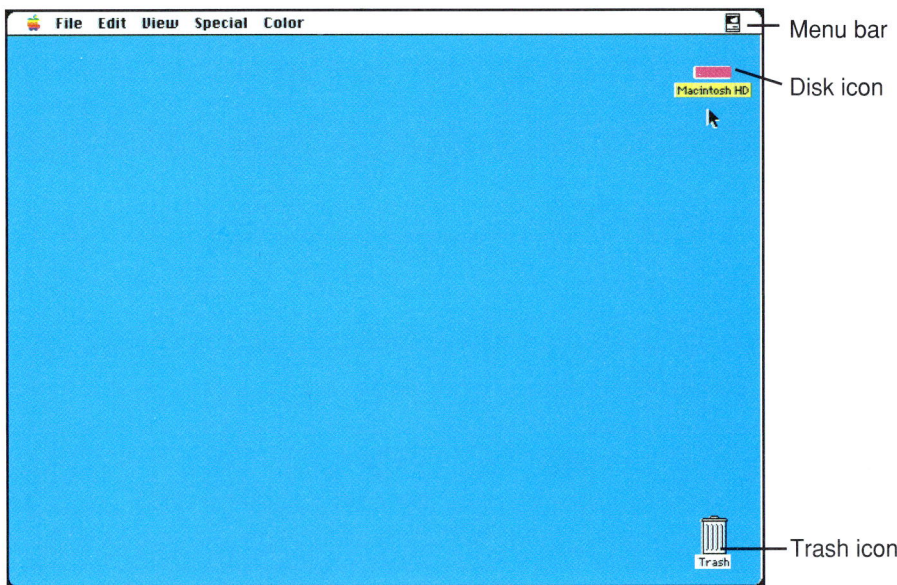

Three items always appear on the Desktop:

- Disk icon
- Trash can icon
- Menu bar

As discussed in the section *Understanding Your Computer System*, you can use two types of disks: floppy disks and hard disks. The Macintosh uses a different icon to represent each. In the following figure, you see icons for both a hard disk (named "Macintosh HD") and a floppy disk (named "Data Disk"):

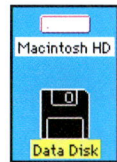

The Trash can icon can contain items that you want to throw away. You probably have a trash can in your office. Well, you also have one on the Desktop, and it serves a similar purpose. You drag the item that you want to throw away to the Trash can icon.

You use the menu bar to select commands.

Selecting a Menu Command

The *menu bar* contains the names of the menus— , File, Edit, View, and Special. (If you are using System 7, your menu bar will look a little different.)

To view a menu, point to the name in the menu bar, press and hold the mouse button. The menu does not stay on-screen unless you keep the mouse button depressed.

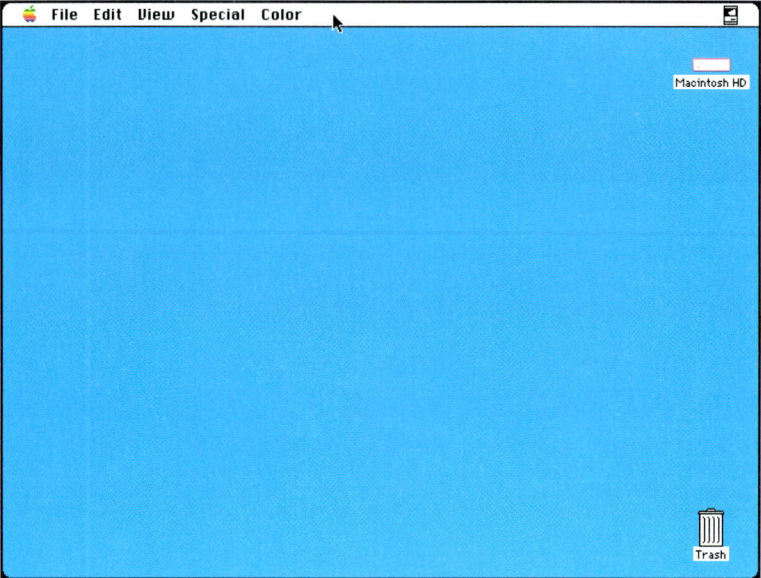

To select a menu command, open the menu and then drag the mouse down through the list of commands until the one you want is highlighted.

Then release the mouse button. The command is activated. (You will know that the command has been activated because it will flash. If it doesn't flash, try again.)

If you don't want to select a command, just drag the mouse off the menu.

If you go past the command you want, drag up until you highlight the command.

The menus tell you other information:

- If an option is grayed, it cannot be selected at that time.
- If an option has a shortcut key, the shortcut is listed on the menu.

- If a command is followed by an ellipsis (...), you must specify additional options before the command can be activated. In this case, a dialog box appears. The dialog box might prompt you to enter text, make a choice about options, or confirm an operation.

Tip: Most Macintosh programs use similar menus. To learn a new program, take a look at the menus. You already might have used the same or similar commands in a different program.

Working with Windows

If you open a disk, the contents appear in a window on-screen. If you run an application, it creates a window for you to work in. If you create a document, it appears in a window.

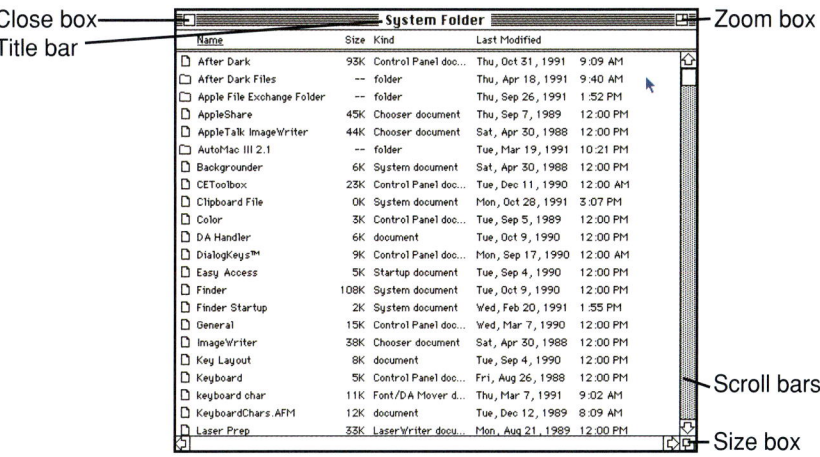

Each window has several standard items:

title bar. The bar that appears at the top of the window and contains the name of the window. Usually, the window name is the name of the document or folder that is open. Horizontal stripes appear in the active window. (You can have more than one window open at one time.)

close box. The square box in the upper left corner of the title bar. To close the window, you can click on this box.

The Basics

zoom box. The small box on top of a larger box in the upper right corner of the window. Click on the box to enlarge the window. Click on it again to restore the window to its previous size. See *TASK: Zoom a window*.

scroll bars. The bars that appear along the right and bottom of some windows. If the scroll bar is white, the entire contents of the window are displayed. If the scroll bar is gray, more items appear outside the window. See *TASK: Scroll a window* to learn to display these hidden items.

size box. The small box within a box in the lower right corner of the title bar. Drag this box to change the size and shape of the window. See TASK: *Resize a window*.

Taking Care of the Macintosh

Take care of the Macintosh hardware (everything you can see and touch) the same way you would care for your TV or VCR. Don't feed it, water it, drop it, or expose it to extreme heat or cold.

Take care of your Macintosh software the same way you would care for audio or video cassettes. Don't leave them in the heat, don't spill anything on them, don't open the metal shutter, and keep them away from magnets. Keep in mind that all electrical equipment puts out a magnetic field. This means the telephone, the electric pencil sharpener, and even the Macintosh. Of course, you don't have to keep your phone in a desk drawer—just don't keep floppy disks near the phone.

Finally, always turn off your machine properly. Close all applications, and be sure that the Desktop appears on-screen. Then use the Shut Down command. (See *TASK: Shut down the Macintosh*.)

Do not turn off your Macintosh when you are using an application:

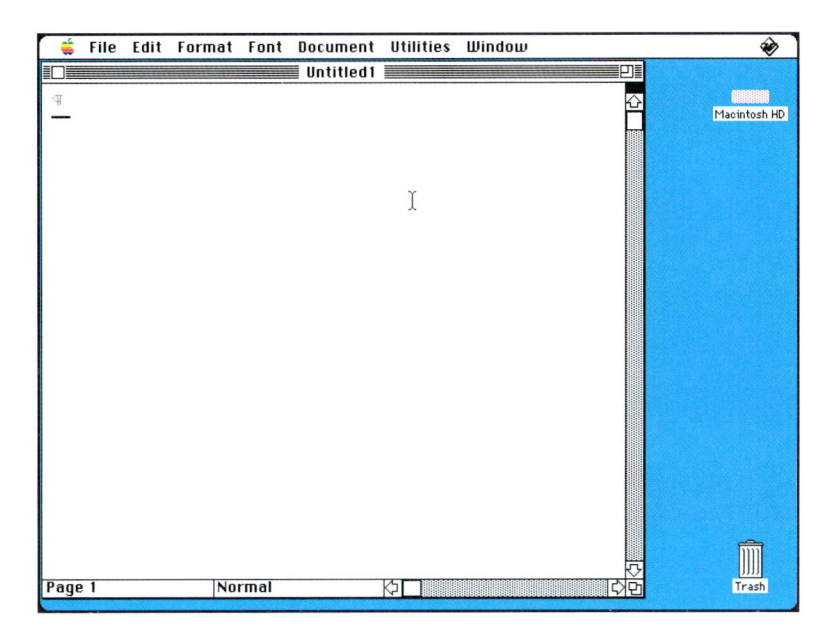

Do turn off your Macintosh when you have closed all applications and the Desktop appears on-screen:

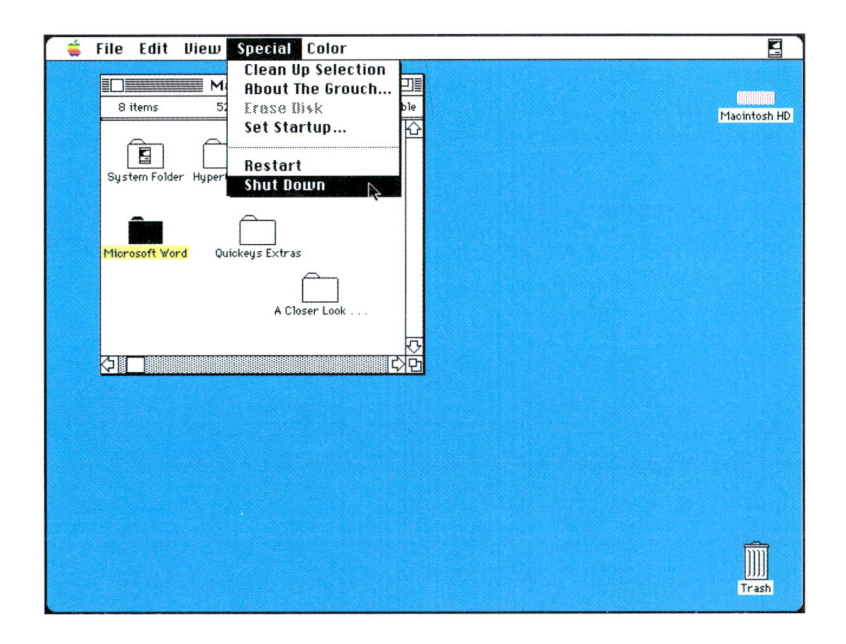

The Basics

29

Understanding Key Terms

As a checkpoint after reading this section, you should understand the following terms.

application. A computer program used for a particular task—such as word processing. In most cases, the terms *program*, *software*, and *application* mean the same thing and can be used interchangeably.

click. The action of pressing and releasing the mouse button.

Desktop. The on-screen work area of the Macintosh.

document. A generic term used to describe what you create with applications. A document can be a letter, a picture, a worksheet—any item that you create with an application.

double-click. The action of pressing the mouse button twice in rapid succession.

drag. The action of pointing to an item, and then pressing and holding down the mouse button as you move the mouse.

file. The various individual reports, memos, databases, and letters that you store on your hard drive (or disk) for future use. Also called a *document*.

Finder. Part of the Macintosh operating system that keeps the Desktop organized.

folder. An item on the Desktop that stores icons of files and other folders.

hardware. The physical parts of the Macintosh—the screen, the keyboard, the mouse, and so on.

icon. An on-screen picture that represents a file, folder, or application program.

menu bar. A list of menu names at the top of the screen.

program. A set of instructions that tells a computer what to do. A *program* is the same as an *application*.

software. Another term for computer programs or applications. You run software on your hardware.

System Folder. The folder that contains the files necessary to start and use the Macintosh.

title bar. The horizontal bar at the top of a window; the title bar contains the name of the window.

Trash can icon. An icon (in the shape of a trash can) used to delete files, folders, and applications.

window. A rectangular area on-screen in which you view an application or a document.

Task/Review

Working with Disks and Windows

Viewing the Desktop

Working with Folders

Working with Documents and Applications

Working with Accessories

Working with HyperCard Stacks

Easy Macintosh

Alphabetical Listing of Tasks

Add a new address card 154
Add a note to an address card 160
Add a note to an appointment card 174
Add an appointment..170
Arrange icons 74
Change the alert sound 138
Change the date..134
Change the Desktop pattern 130
Change the speaker volume 132
Change the time 136
Close a window 46
Copy a document to another disk..122
Copy a document to another folder...120
Copy a floppy disk to another floppy disk 68
Copy a folder 100
Copy the contents of a floppy disk to a hard disk........................66
Create a new folder 94
Delete a document 124
Delete a folder 102
Delete an address card 164
Delete an appointment..178
Display a different address card 156
Display a different appointment date...168
Display a special character...146
Display information about a disk 62
Display information about a document 110
Display information about a folder 98
Display the time..140
Duplicate a document 114
Edit an address card 162
Edit an appointment card...176
Eject a disk 58

Empty the Trash	106
Erase a disk	64
Find a document	126
Find an address card	158
Find an appointment card	172
Initialize a disk	56
Insert a disk	54
Lock a document	112
Move a document to another folder	118
Move a window	48
Move an icon	72
Open a disk icon	44
Open a folder	76
Open the Addresses With Audio stack	150
Open the Appointments With Audio stack	166
Quit HyperCard	152
Rename a disk icon	60
Rename a document	116
Rename a folder	96
Resize a window	50
Restart the Macintosh	42
Retrieve an item from the Trash	104
Scroll a window	80
Select a window	78
Set an alarm	142
Shut down the Macintosh	40
Start the Macintosh	38
Use the calculator	144
View a window by date	86
View a window by kind	90
View a window by name	84
View a window by size	88
View a window by small icon	82
Zoom a window	52

Working with Disks and Windows

This section covers the following tasks:
Start the Macintosh
Shut down the Macintosh
Restart the Macintosh
Open a disk icon
Close a window
Move a window
Resize a window
Zoom a window
Insert a disk
Initialize a disk
Eject a disk
Rename a disk icon
Display information about a disk
Erase a disk
Copy the contents of a floppy disk to a hard disk
Copy a floppy disk to another floppy disk

TASK

Start the Macintosh

before

Oops!
If the Macintosh does not turn on, make sure that it is plugged in and that all cables are connected.

Press the On switch.

Your On switch might appear in a different location, depending on the Macintosh model that you have. On some Macintoshes, the power switch is located on the keyboard; on others, it is located on the back of the system unit. Press the On switch to turn on the monitor, if necessary.

You see the Happy Macintosh Face, the Welcome to the Macintosh screen, and then the Desktop.

On the Desktop, you see the hard disk icon, the Trash can icon, and the menu bar. For a more complete discussion of the Desktop, see the Basics part of this book.

after

Press the **On Switch**.

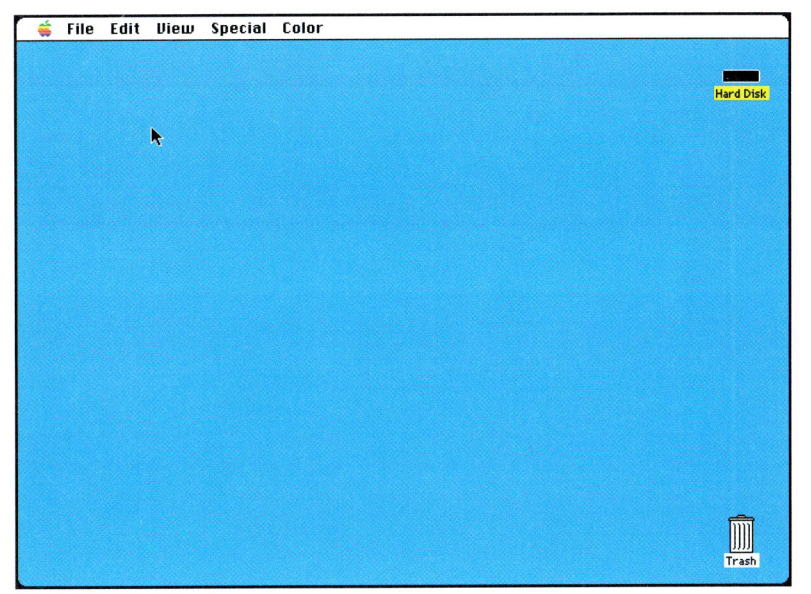

Sad Macintosh face appears?
If you see a sad Macintosh face, contact your dealer. You might have a problem with your equipment.

REVIEW

To start the Macintosh

See something different?
The Macintosh remembers how the Desktop appeared the last time you used it. If you have opened or rearranged windows, you will see a different arrangement than the one shown in the After screen.

Working with Disks and Windows

39

TASK

Shut down the Macintosh

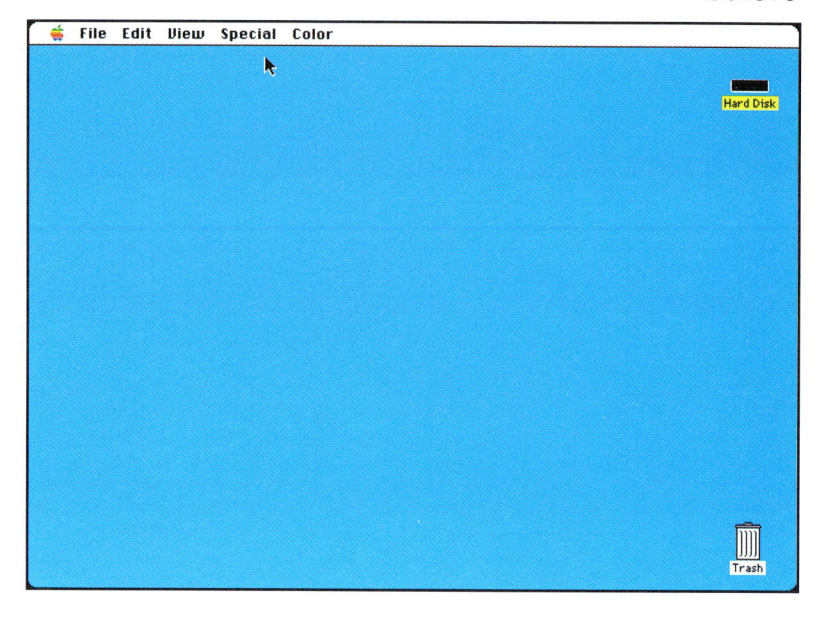

before

Oops!
If you change your mind, just turn your Macintosh on again.

1. Click on **Special** in the menu bar; hold down the mouse button.

   This step opens the Special menu. You see a list of commands.

2. Drag down until you highlight **Shut Down**.

   This step selects the Shut Down command. (The After screen shows this step.)

3. Release the mouse button.

   Depending on the model you have, your Macintosh turns off after this step, or you see a message `You may now switch off your Macintosh safely.` If this message appears, follow step 4.

4. Turn off the Macintosh.

   The power switch is on the back of the system unit or on the keyboard, depending on the type of Macintosh you have. This step completes the shut down operation.

after

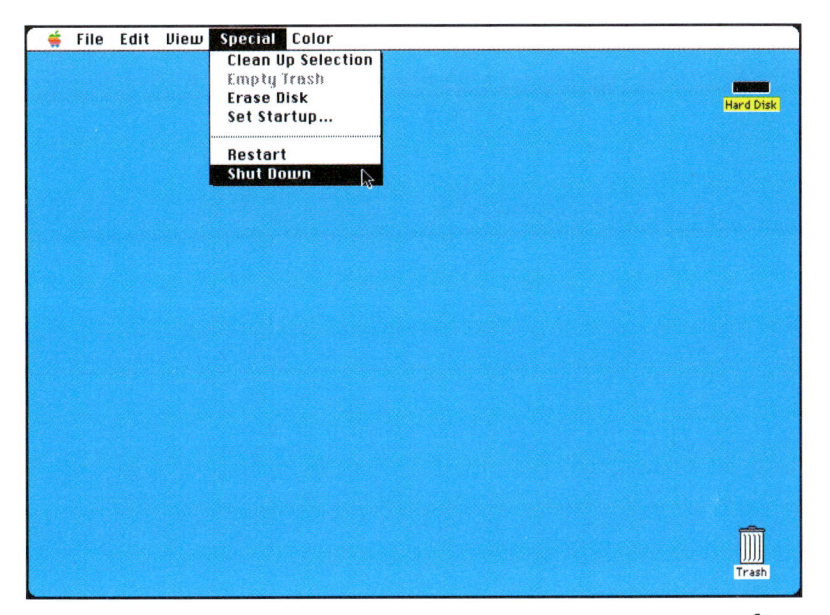

Why use Shut Down?
The Macintosh keeps track of information about your Desktop. You must use the Shut Down command so that the Macintosh can do some "housekeeping" before it shuts down. Don't turn off the Macintosh in the middle of an application or you might damage your software.

REVIEW

1. From the **Special** menu, select **Shut Down**.

2. If you see a message telling you that you may turn off the Macintosh, turn off the Macintosh.

To shut down the Macintosh

Working with Disks and Windows

41

TASK

Restart the Macintosh

before

Oops!
If you don't want to restart the Macintosh, drag the mouse off the menu. Do not release the mouse button until the pointer is off the menu.

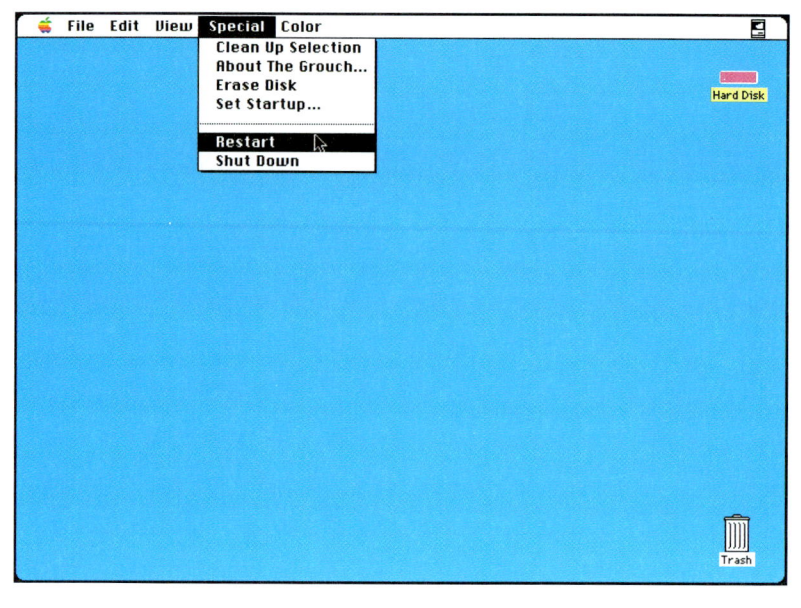

1. Click on **Special** in the menu bar; hold down the mouse button.
   This step opens the Special menu. You see a list of commands.

2. Drag down until you highlight **Restart**.
   This step selects the Restart command. (The Before screen shows this step.)

3. **Release the mouse button**
   The Macintosh is restarted.

Easy **Macintosh**

after

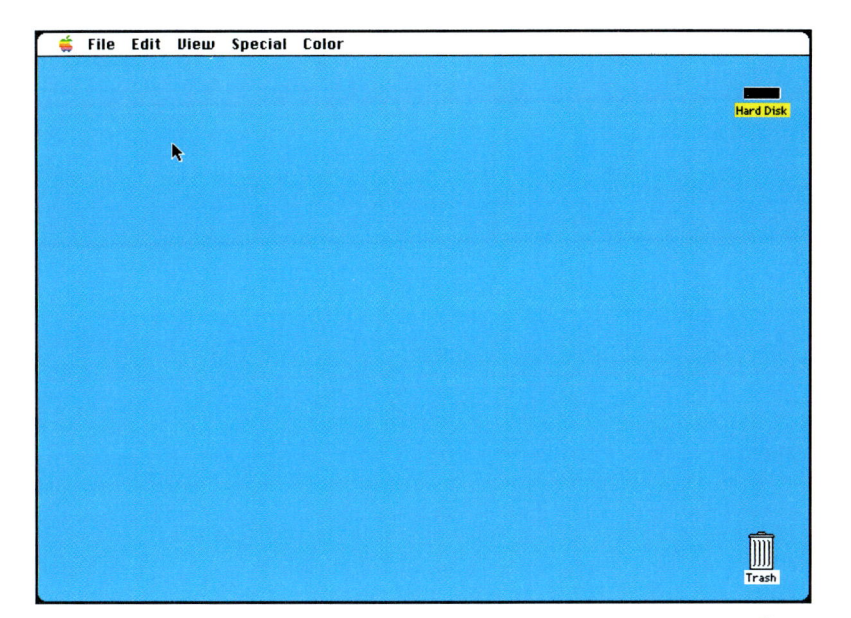

From the **Special** menu, select **Restart**.

Why restart?
When you make certain changes (install a new application or add an item to your System folder), you need to restart so that the Macintosh can make note of these changes.

REVIEW

To restart the Macintosh

Working with Disks and Windows

43

TASK

Open a disk icon

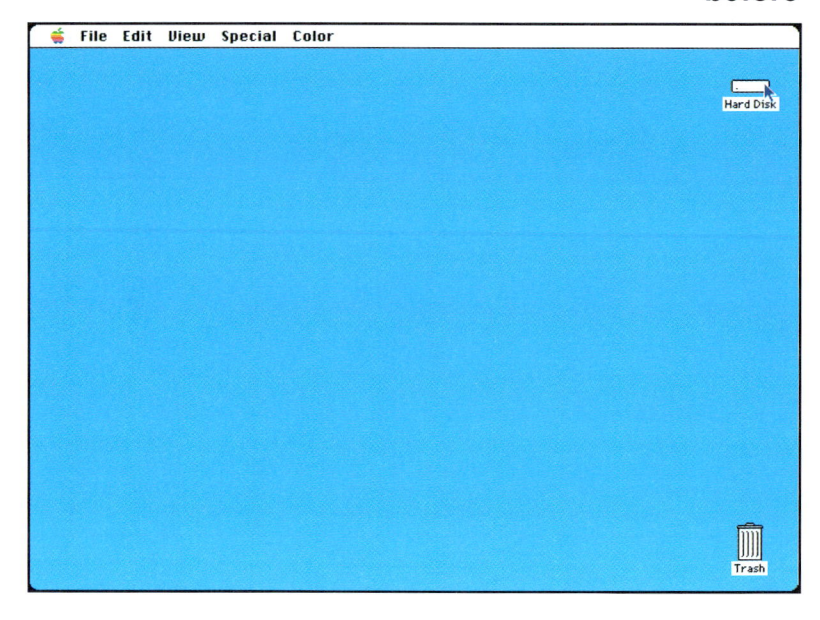

before

Oops!
To close the window, see
TASK: Close a window.

1. Position the mouse pointer on the disk icon named **Hard Disk**.

   This step points to the icon that you want to open. Your hard disk might have a different name. In this case, point to that icon.

2. Double-click the mouse button.

   Double-clicking means to press the mouse button twice in rapid succession. This step opens a disk window that shows the contents of the disk. The name of the window, Hard Disk, appears in the title bar. If icons appear (rather than file names), the title bar displays the number of items in the window and the size of the items appear under the title bar. The amount of space remaining on disk also appears.

   The disk in the After screen contains the System Folder, HyperCard, a Data folder, and Microsoft Word. Your disk might contain different items.

   Icons are usually displayed to indicate each item on the disk. You also can display item names instead of icons (see *TASK: View a window by name*).

   You use this same procedure to display the contents of hard disks and floppy disks.

Easy **Macintosh**

after

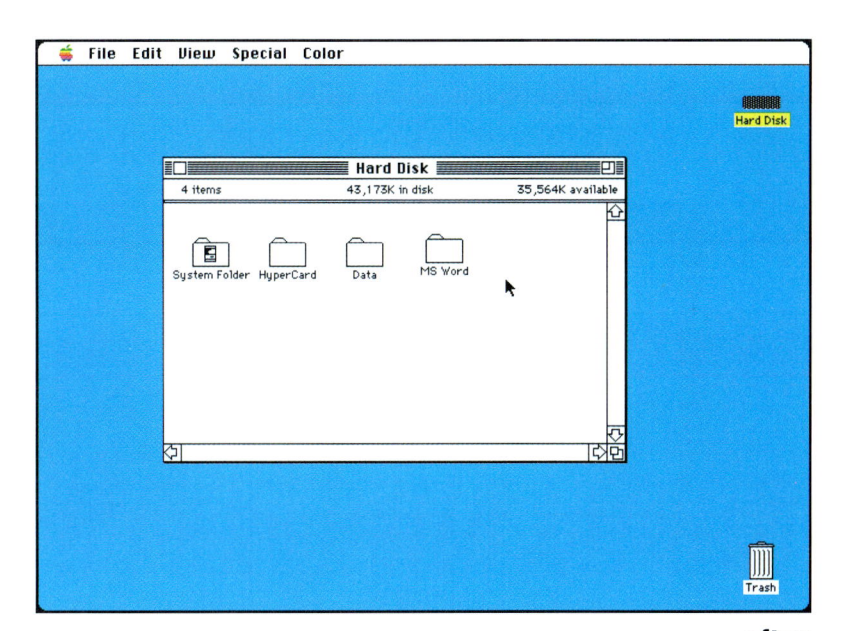

Rearrange the window
You can move, resize, and scroll the window. See later tasks in this section.

REVIEW

1. Point to the disk icon.
2. Double-click the mouse button.

To open a disk icon

Working with Disks and Windows

TASK

Close a window

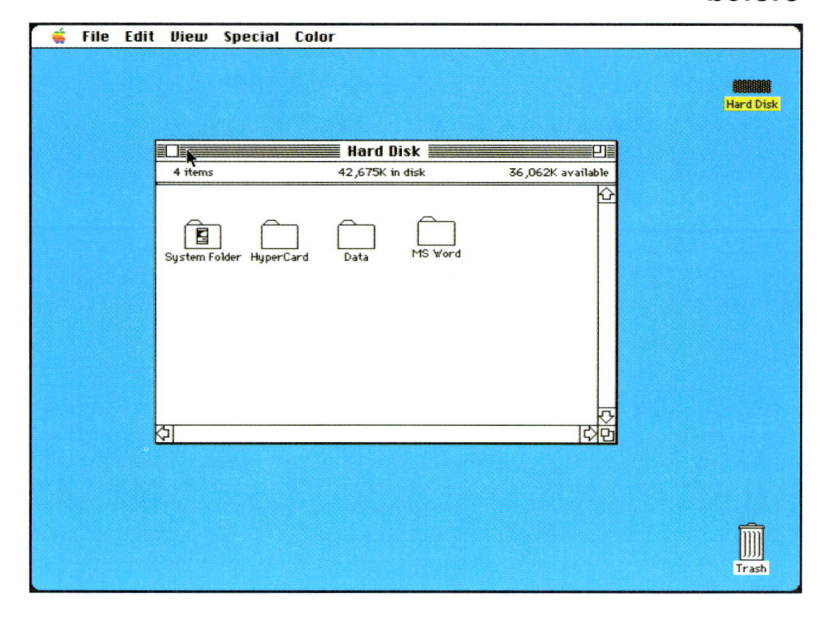

before

Oops!
To reopen the window, double-click on the disk icon.

1. Point to the **Hard Disk** icon.

   This step selects the icon that you want to open. (If you already have a window open, you can skip this step and step 2.)

2. Double-click the mouse button.

   This step opens a disk window that displays the contents of the disk.

3. Click on the **close box**.

   The close box is the small square in the title bar of the window. This step closes the window.

   Use this procedure to close any type of window—a disk window, a document window, a folder window, and so on. When you close the hard disk window, you see just the Desktop. When you close a folder window, you see the disk window. When you close a folder within a folder, you see the previous folder window. Windows are stacked on-screen in the order that you opened them.

after

Click on the **close box**.

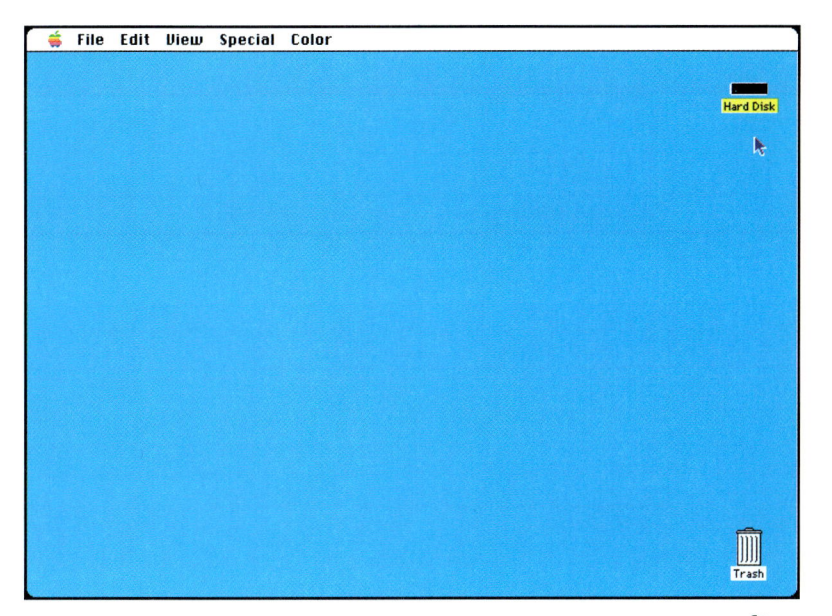

Try this Tip
To close all windows, press and hold the Option key; then click on the close box.

REVIEW

To close a window

Working with Disks and Windows

47

TASK

Move a window

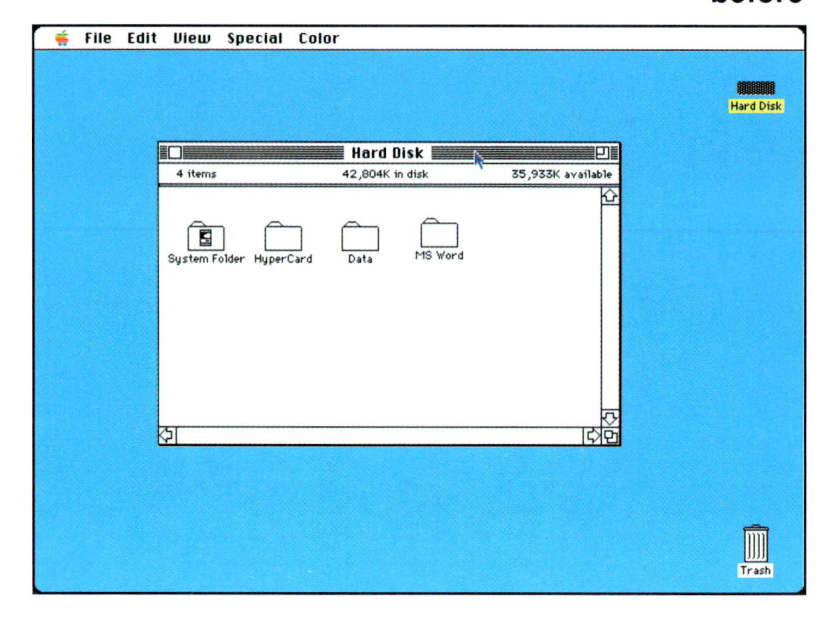

before

Oops!
Follow this same procedure to move the window back to its original location.

1. Double-click on the **Hard Disk** icon.

   If you already have a window open, you don't need to follow this step. Your hard disk might be named differently; double-click on the icon for your hard disk.

   This step opens a disk window that displays the contents of the disk.

2. Point to the title bar of the window.

   The title bar is the lined row at the top of the window.

3. Click and hold the mouse button.

   This step selects the window.

4. Drag until the window is in the upper left corner of the Desktop.

   As you drag, you can see an outline of the window.

5. Release the mouse button.

   This step completes the move. The window appears at the new location.

after

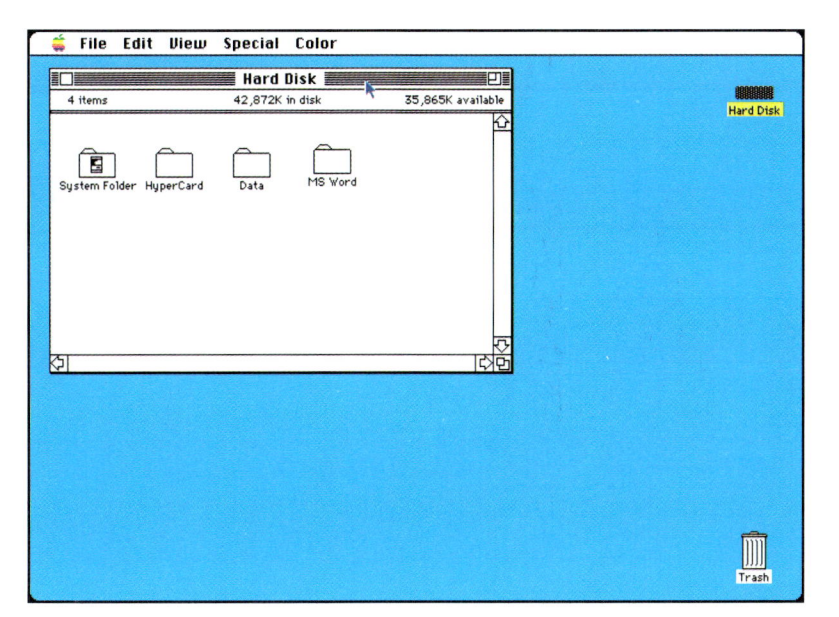

Outline disappears?
If the outline disappears, you are attempting to move the window off the screen. Continue holding the mouse button and move back into the screen. The outline will reappear.

REVIEW

To move a window

1. Point to the title bar of the window you want to move.
2. Click and hold the mouse button.
3. Drag the window to the new location.
4. Release the mouse button.

Working with Disks and Windows

TASK

Resize a window

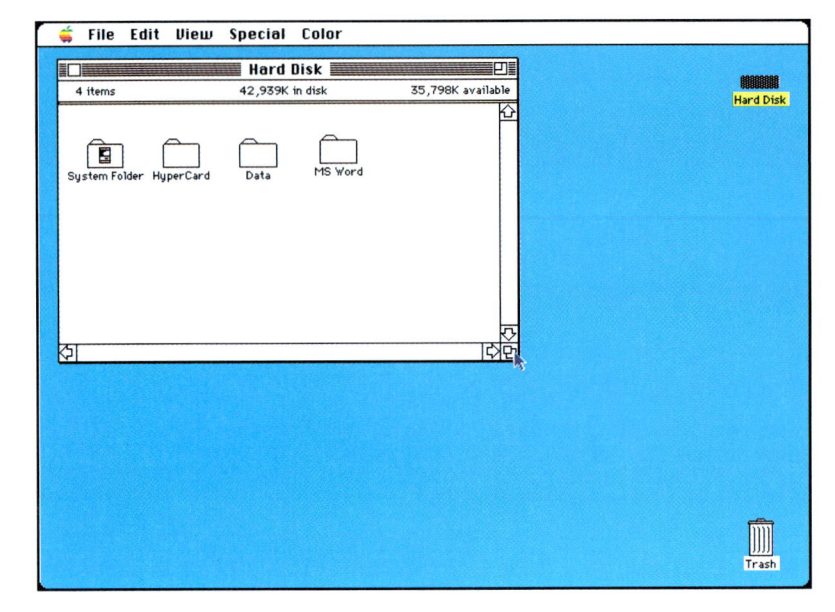

before

Oops!
Follow this same procedure to resize the window again.

1. Double-click on the **Hard Disk** icon.

   If you already have a window open, you don't need to follow this step. Your hard disk might be named differently; double-click on the icon for your hard disk.

   This step opens a disk window that displays the contents of the disk.

2. Position the mouse pointer on the **size box**.

   The size box is in the lower right corner of the window. The icon is a smaller box on top of a larger box.

3. Click and hold the mouse button.

   This step selects the size box.

4. Drag up until the window is about half its original size.

   You see an outline of the window moving with the mouse pointer.

5. Release the mouse button.

   The window is resized.

   Windows have a size limit. If you are resizing a window and the outline stops moving, you have reached the limit of the window.

Easy **Macintosh**

after

1. Click on the **size box** and hold down the mouse button.
2. Drag the window until it is the size you want.
3. Release the mouse button.

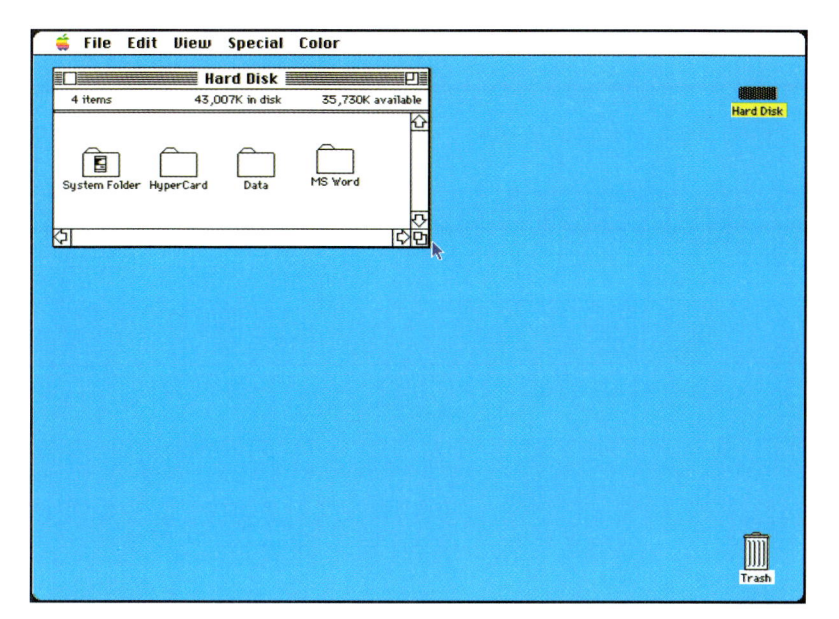

Zoom the window
To zoom the window (enlarge it to almost full-screen size), see *TASK: Zoom a window.*

REVIEW

To resize a window

Working with Disks and Windows

TASK

Zoom a window

before

Oops!
Click on the zoom box again to return to the previous window size.

1. Double-click on the **Hard Disk** icon.

   If you already have a window open, you don't need to follow this step. Your hard disk might be named differently; double-click on the icon for your hard disk.

   This step opens a disk window that displays the contents of the disk.

2. Click on the **zoom box**.

   The zoom box is in the upper right corner of the window—in the title bar. It is represented by a small box within a larger box.

   This step enlarges the window to fill almost the entire screen.

after

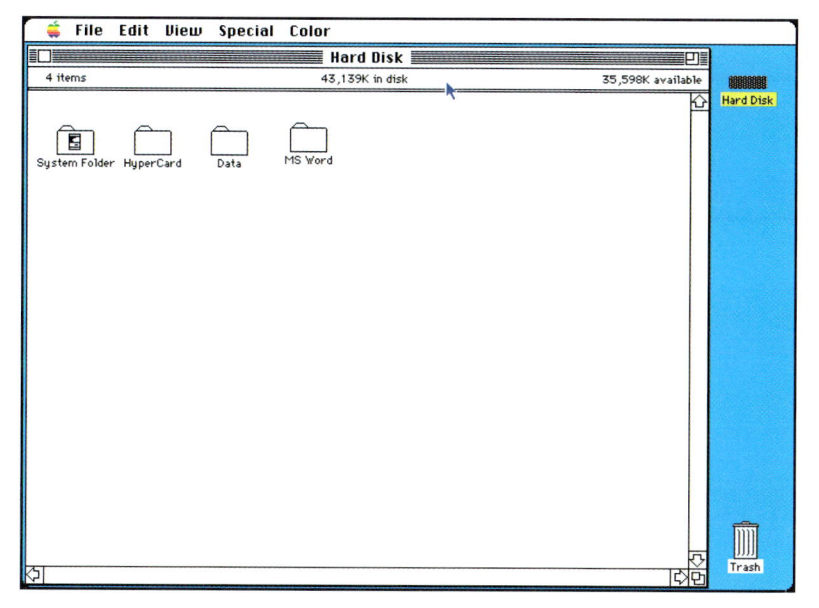

REVIEW

Click on the **zoom box**.

To zoom a window

Working with Disks and Windows

53

TASK

Insert a disk

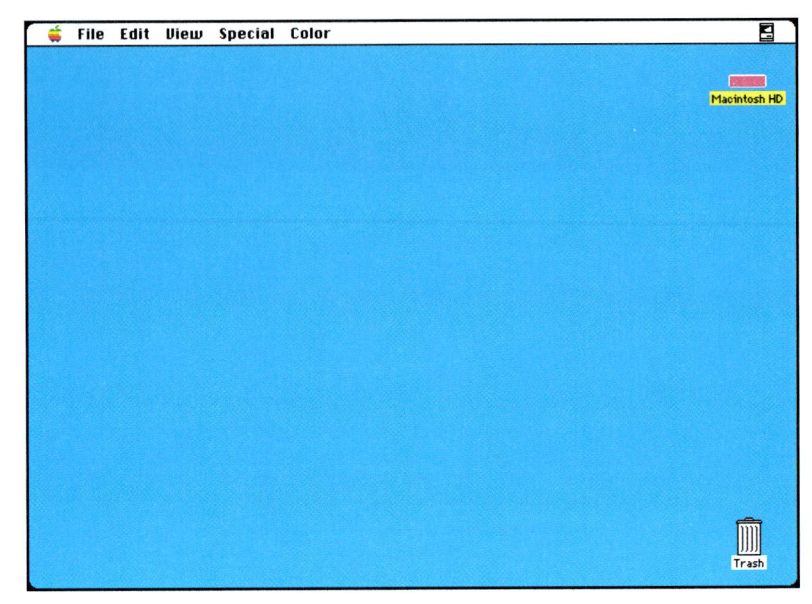

before

[Macintosh desktop screenshot showing File, Edit, View, Special, Color menus with Macintosh HD and Trash icons]

1. **Hold the disk so that you can see the label and the metal part of the disk is pointing towards the computer.**

   Just as you should not insert a video cassette tape upside down into your VCR, you should not insert a computer disk upside down. Be sure to insert the disk with the label facing up. Some disks have an arrow on them that indicates the direction to insert the disk.

2. **Insert the disk into the drive.**

   You hear a click and the disk icon appears on-screen. The icon is darkened because it is selected.

   Open the icon like any other disk icon—double-click on it.

   Never force a disk into the drive.

Oops!
If you see a round metal circle in the center of the disk, the disk is upside down. Turn the disk over before inserting it into the Macintosh.

Easy **Macintosh**

after

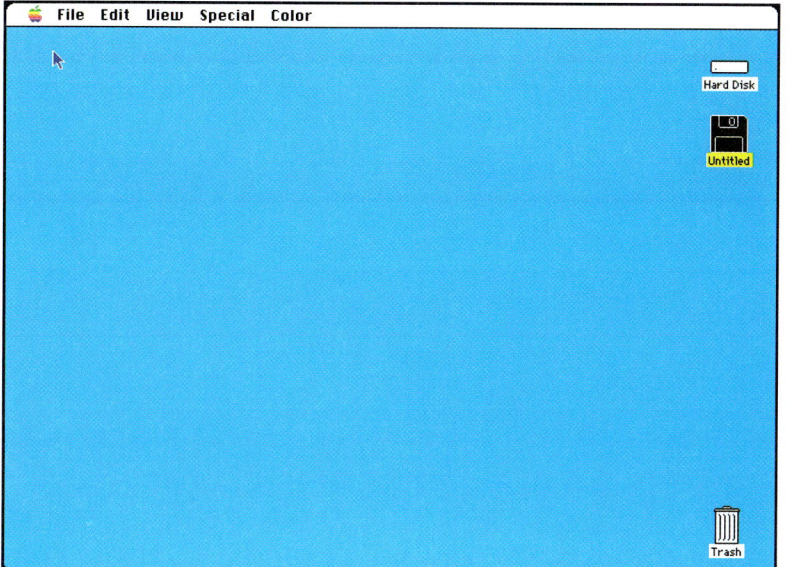

Not a Macintosh disk?
If the disk is not a Macintosh disk or has not been formatted (prepared for use), a message appears in a dialog box on-screen. Click on the Eject button to eject the disk. To format the disk, see *TASK: Initialize a disk*.

REVIEW

1. Hold the disk label up.
2. Insert the disk into the computer.

To insert a disk

Working with Disks and Windows

55

TASK

Initialize a disk

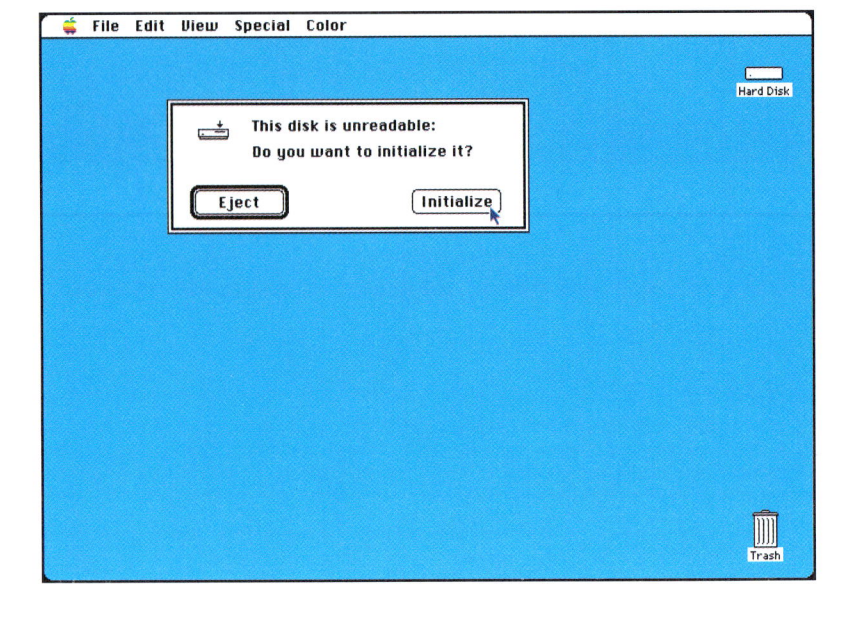

before

Oops!
If you change your mind, click on Eject for step 2 or click on Cancel for step 3.

1. **Insert a blank disk into the drive.**
   For help with this step, see *TASK: Insert a disk*. You see the message `This disk is unreadable: Do you want to initialize it?`

   Depending on the type of disk that you have inserted, you see these choices:

   `Eject` or `Initialize`

   or

   `Eject,` `One-Sided,` or `Two-Sided`

2. **If you see the first message, click on Initialize. If you see the second message, click on Two-Sided.**
   This step tells the Macintosh to initialize the disk. You see the message `This process will erase all information on this disk.`

3. **Click on Erase.**
   This step confirms that you want to erase the disk. You see the message `Please name this disk:.` The current name, Untitled, is highlighted.

4. **Type Reports.**
   This is the name that you want to assign the disk. The name can be up to 27 characters long; do not use the colon (:) in the name.

Easy **Macintosh**

after

5. Click on **OK**.

   This step confirms the name and starts the initialization process. You see the messages `Formatting disk...`, `Verifying Format...`, and `Creating Directory...`

   When the process is complete, the disk icon appears on the Desktop.

REVIEW

To initialize a disk

1. Insert a blank disk.

2. Click on **Initialize** or **Two-Sided**, depending on the message that appears.

3. Click on **Erase**.

4. Type a name for the disk.

5. Click on **OK**.

Be Careful!
When you initialize a disk, you erase all information on that disk. Of course, if the disk is blank when you insert it, erasing information is not a problem.

Erase a disk
If you want to initialize a disk that has already been initialized once, see *TASK: Erase a disk*.

TASK

Eject a disk

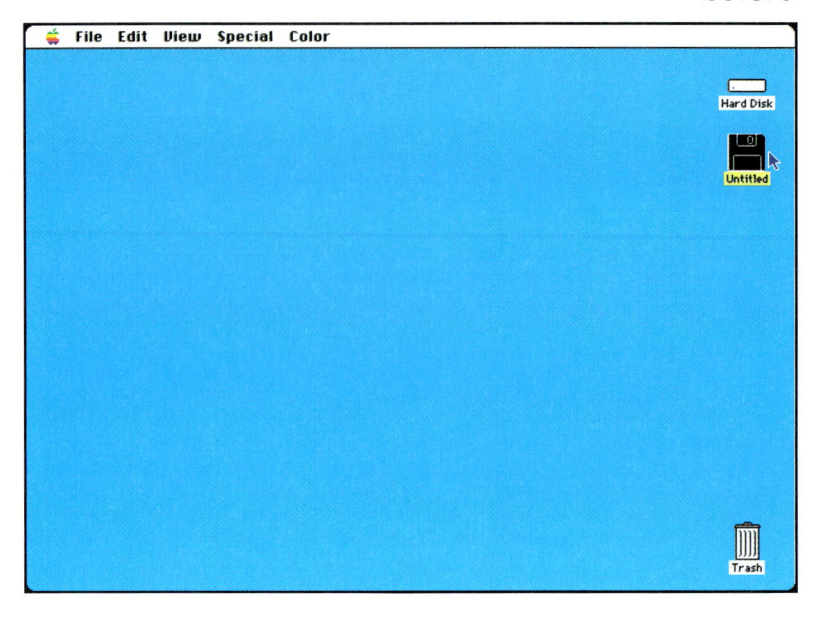

before

Oops!
You must drag the floppy disk icon to the Trash can icon so that the Trash can icon darkens. If it does not darken, you only have moved the floppy disk icon; you have not thrown it away.

1. Click on the floppy disk icon.

   This step selects the disk; the icon darkens.

2. Hold down the mouse button and drag the floppy disk icon to the Trash can icon.

   An outline of the disk moves on-screen as you move the disk icon. When the disk icon is in the proper location (on the Trash can icon), the Trash can icon darkens, and the floppy disk is ejected. This step does not erase the disk. It simply ejects the disk.

Easy **Macintosh**

after

1. Click on the disk icon.

2. Hold down the mouse button and drag the icon to the **Trash can** icon.

Use another method
You also can select Eject from the File menu to eject the disk. This command ejects the disk, but leaves a shadow of the disk icon on-screen. Information about the disk is still in memory.

REVIEW

To eject a disk

Try a shortcut
Press the ⌘-E keyboard shortcut to eject a disk.

Working with Disks and Windows

TASK

Rename a disk icon

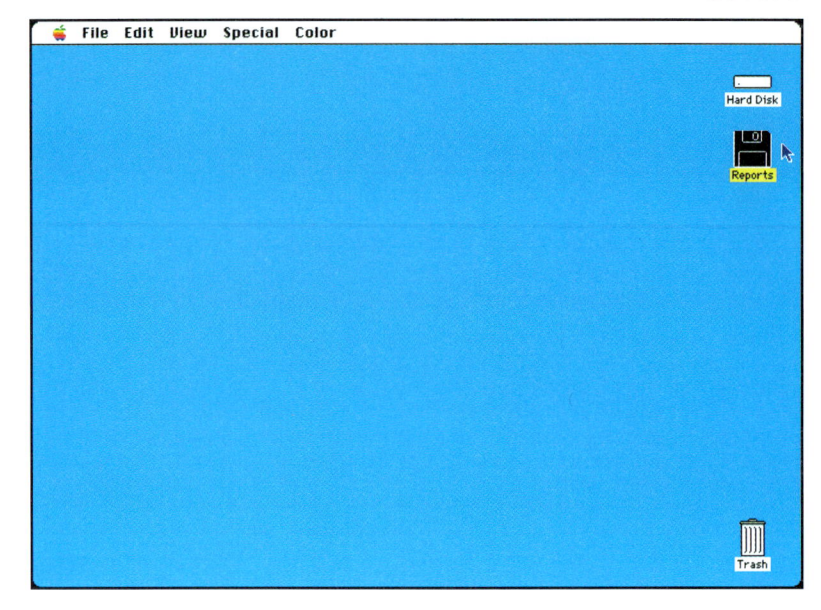

before

Oops!
Follow this same procedure to change the disk back to its original name.

1. Insert the **Reports** disk.

   If this disk is already inserted, skip this step. If you don't have this disk (see *TASK: Initialize a disk*), insert another disk.

2. Click on the disk icon.*

   This step selects the disk icon. The icon darkens.

3. Type **Reports 92**.

   When you start typing, the previous name is deleted, and the new name appears under the disk.

   This is the name you want to assign to the disk. The name can be up to 27 characters; do not use the colon (:) in the name.

4. Press **Return**.

   This step confirms the name. The disk icon remains selected.

*CLICK ON THE "NAME PORTION" OF THE ICON!

Easy **Macintosh**

after

1. Click on the disk icon.
2. Type the new name.
3. Press **Return**.

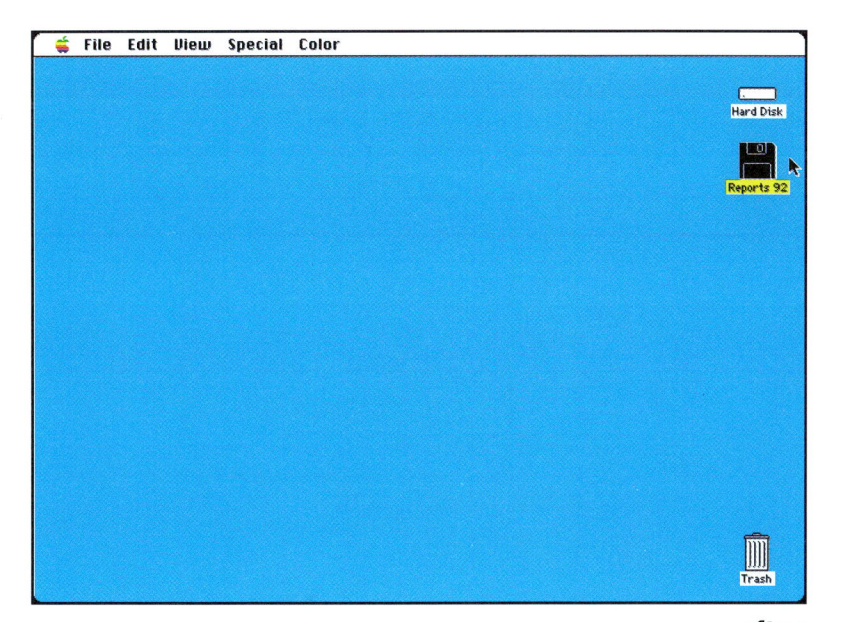

Rename the hard disk
You can follow this same procedure to rename the hard disk icon.

REVIEW

To rename a disk icon

TASK

Display information about a disk

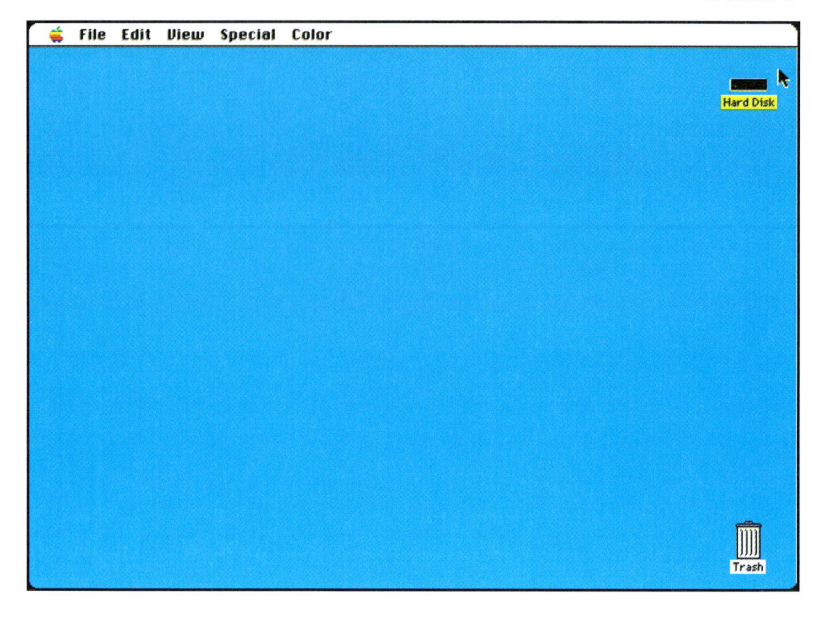

before

Oops!
Click on the close box to close the Info window.

1. Click on the **Hard Disk icon**.

   This step selects the hard disk icon. Your hard disk might be named differently; double-click on the icon for your hard disk.

2. Click on **File** in the menu bar and hold down the mouse button.

   This step opens the File menu. You see a list of File commands.

3. Drag down until you highlight **Get Info**.

   This step selects the Get Info command.

4. Release the mouse button.

   You see an Info window on-screen that displays the following information:

Kind	The kind of item selected; in this case, a disk.
Size	The size in bytes (characters) and kilobytes (K) and the number of files on the Macintosh.
Where	The location of the selected item; in this case, the ID number of the disk.
Created	The date that the disk was created.
Modified	The date that the disk was last modified.

Easy **Macintosh**

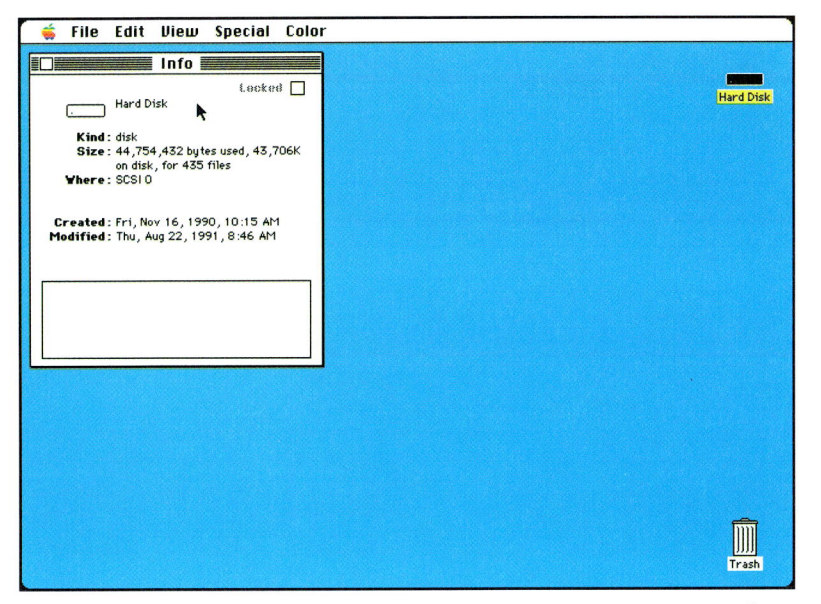

after

The insertion point is in a comment box at the bottom of the window. If you want, you can type a comment.

5. Click on the **close box**.
   This step closes the Info window.

Try a shortcut
You also can press the ⌘-I keyboard shortcut to select the Get Info command.

REVIEW

1. Click on the disk icon.
2. From the **File** menu, select **Get Info**.
3. Click on the **close box**.

To display information about a disk

Working with Disks and Windows

63

TASK

Erase a disk

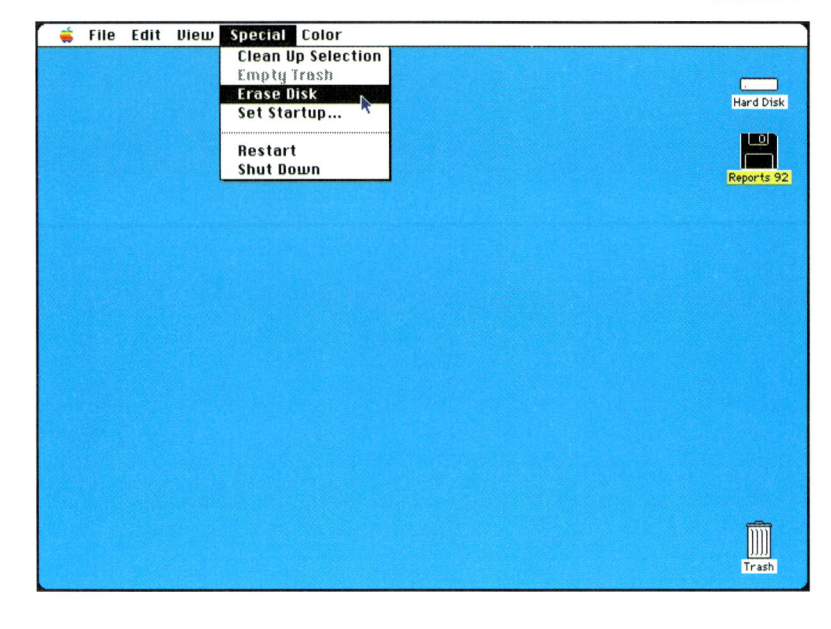

before

Oops!
Click on Cancel for step 6 of the Task section to cancel the procedure.

1. Insert the **Reports 92** disk.

   If the disk is already inserted, skip this step. If you don't have this disk, insert another disk. Be sure that it is a disk you don't need.

2. Click on the **Reports 92** icon.

   This step selects the disk. It darkens on-screen.

3. Click on **Special** in the menu bar; hold down the mouse button.

   This step opens the Special menu. You see a list of Special commands.

4. Drag down until you highlight **Erase Disk**.

   This step selects the Erase Disk command. The Before screen shows this step.

5. Release the mouse button.

   You see a message that says Completely erase disk named "Reports 92" (internal drive)? Depending on the disk type, you see these choices:

   Cancel or Initialize

   or

   Cancel, One-Sided, or Two-Sided

64

Easy Macintosh

after

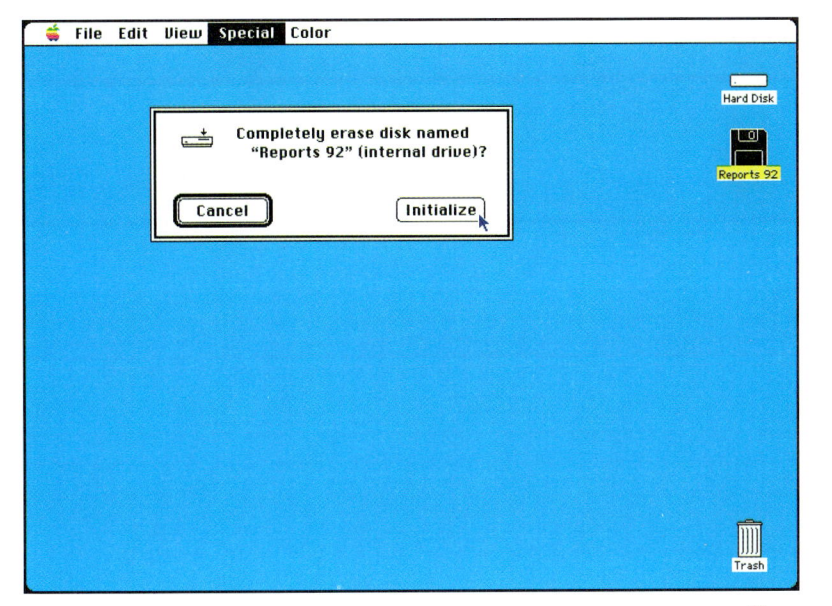

6. Click on **Initialize** or **Two-Sided**, depending on what options appear.

    This step confirms the name and starts the initialization process. You see the messages `Formatting disk...`, `Verifying Format...`, and `Creating Directory...`

    When the process is complete, you see the disk icon on the Desktop.

REVIEW

1. Click on the disk icon.
2. From the **Special** menu, select **Erase Disk**.
3. Click on **Initialize** or **Two-Sided**, depending on the disk type.

Be careful!
Be sure that you want to initialize (erase) the disk. All information on that disk will be lost.

To erase a disk

Working with Disks and Windows

65

TASK

Copy the contents of a floppy disk to a hard disk

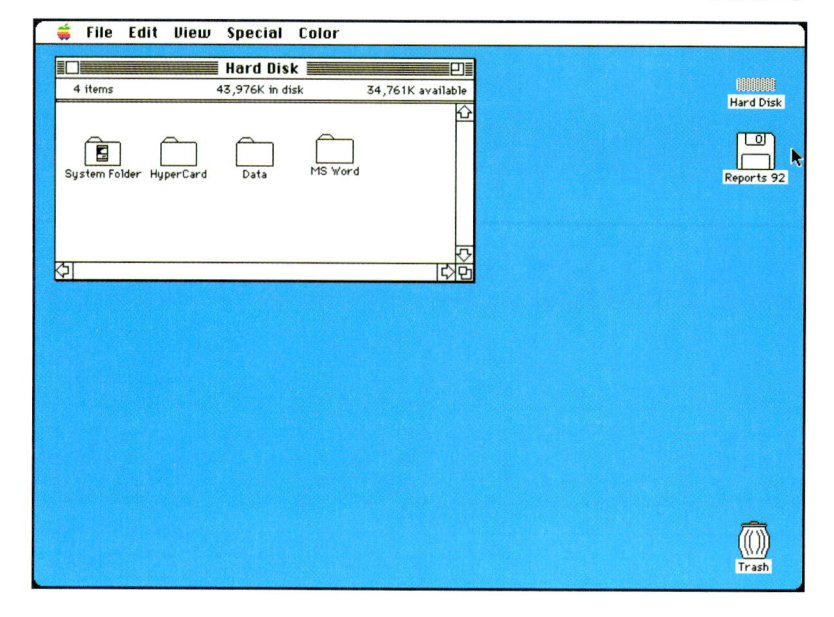

before

Oops!
To cancel the procedure, click on Cancel for step 6 of the Task section.

1. Double-click on the **Hard Disk** icon.

   This step opens the Hard Disk window. Your hard disk might be named differently; double-click on the icon for your hard disk.

   You don't have to open the hard disk window, but doing so will enable you to see the folder that is created.

2. Insert the **Reports 92** disk.

   For help with this step, see *TASK: Insert a disk*. If the disk is already inserted, you can skip this step. If you don't have this disk, insert one that you do have.

3. Click on the **Reports 92** icon; hold down the mouse button.

   This step selects the disk. It darkens on-screen.

4. Drag the disk icon to the **Hard Disk** window.

   This step tells the Macintosh to place the contents of the floppy disk onto the hard disk. As you drag, you see an outline of the disk. Be sure to drag to a blank area of the window. If you drag to a folder, the contents of the disk will be placed in that folder.

5. Release the mouse button.

   You see the message `The two disks are different types, so the contents of "Reports 92" will be placed in a folder on "Hard Disk".`

Easy **Macintosh**

after

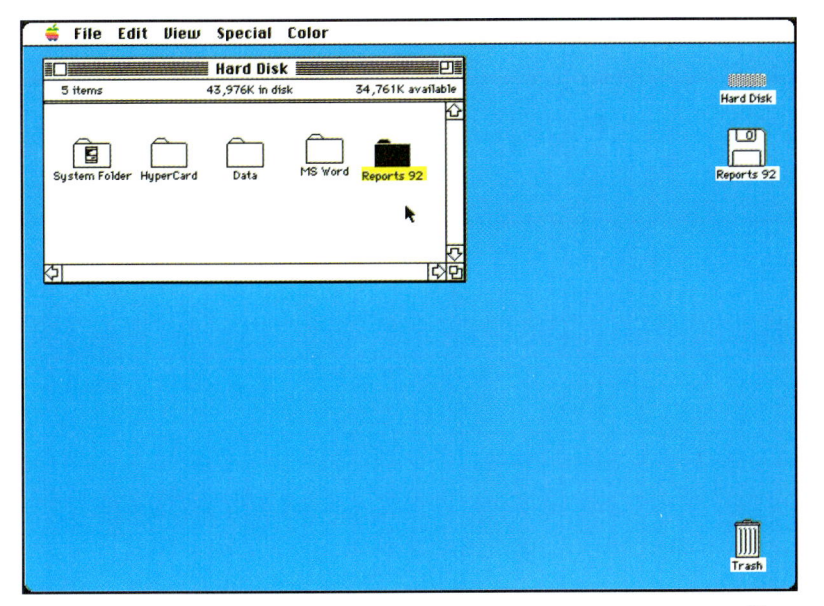

Open the folder
To open the folder that you just placed on the hard disk, see *TASK: Open a folder*.

6. Click on **OK**.

   Clicking on the OK button confirms the copy. You see a progress window at the top of the Desktop. This window tells you how many files are copied and written to disk.

REVIEW

To copy the contents of a floppy disk to a hard disk

1. Open the hard disk window.
2. Insert the floppy disk.
3. Click on the floppy disk icon; hold down the mouse button.
4. Drag the floppy disk icon to the hard disk window.
5. Click on the **OK** button.

Working with Disks and Windows

67

TASK

Copy a floppy disk to another floppy disk

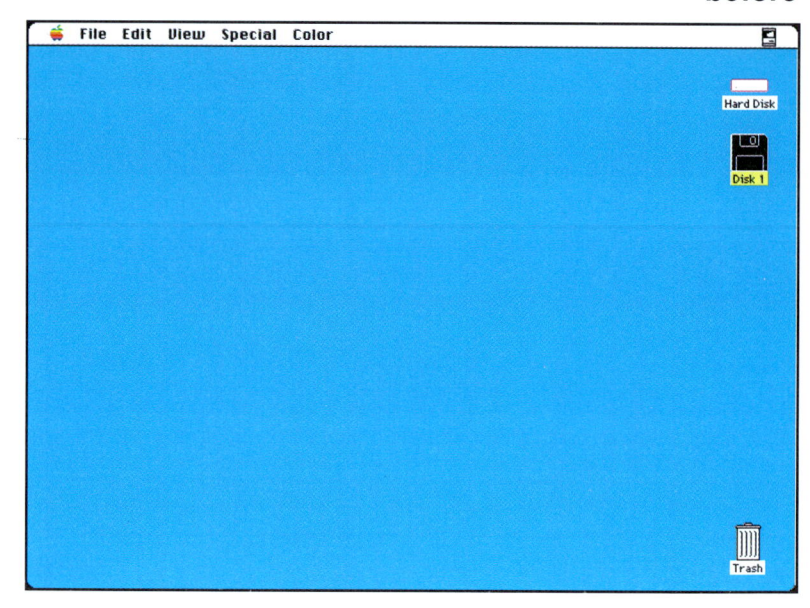

before

Oops!
If you change your mind, click on Cancel for step 5.

1. **Insert the floppy disk that you want to copy to.**

   For help with this step, see *TASK: Insert a disk*. You see the disk icon on-screen.

2. **From the File menu, select Eject.**

   This step ejects the disk, but leaves a shadowed version of the disk icon on-screen. The information about the disk is still in memory.

3. **Insert the disk you want to copy.**

   For help with this step, see *TASK: Insert a disk*. You see the disk icon on-screen.

   This procedure replaces the contents of one disk with the contents of another—it does not just copy and add the contents of one disk to the other. Be sure that you don't need the information on the disk that you are copying to.

4. **Drag the icon for the disk you inserted in step 3 to the icon for the disk you inserted in step 1.**

   This step tells the Macintosh to copy the first disk to the second disk. You see a message that asks whether you are sure you want to completely replace the contents of the second disk with the contents of the first disk.

Easy Macintosh

after

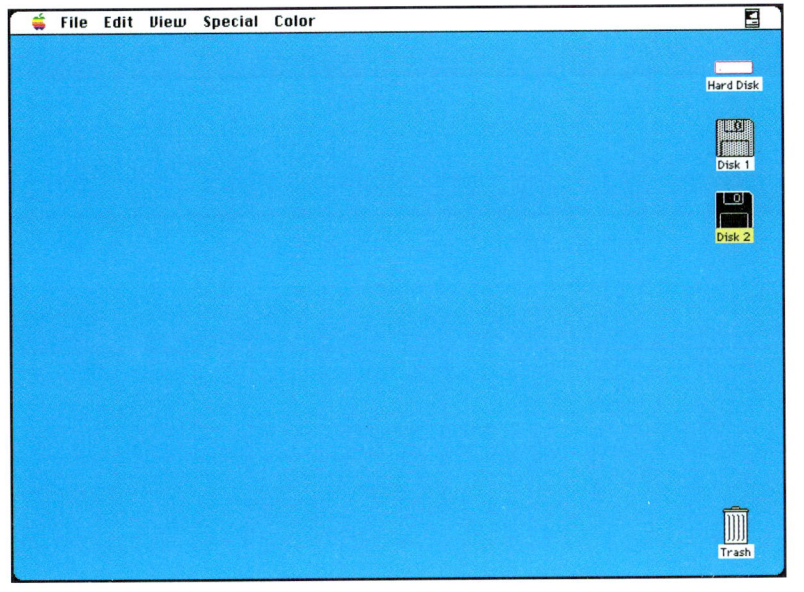

Ejecting the disk
You must use the Eject command to eject the disk. You cannot drag the disk to the Trash can icon to eject it.

5. Click on **OK**.

   Clicking on the OK button confirms the operation. You see a message prompting you to insert the first disk.

6. Insert the disks as requested.

   You are prompted several times to swap the disks. When the disk is copied, you will see icons of both disks on-screen. You can eject the disks. See *TASK: Eject a disk*.

REVIEW

To copy a floppy disk to another floppy disk

1. Insert the disk that you want to copy to.
2. From the **File** menu, select **Eject** to eject the disk.
3. Insert the disk you want to copy.
4. Drag the disk that you inserted in step 3 to the disk that you inserted in step 1.
5. Click on the **OK** button.
6. Swap disks as prompted.

Working with Disks and Windows

Viewing the Desktop

This section covers the following tasks:

Move an icon

Arrange icons

Open a folder

Select a window

Scroll a window

View a window by small icon

View a window by name

View a window by date

View a window by size

View a window by kind

TASK

Move an icon

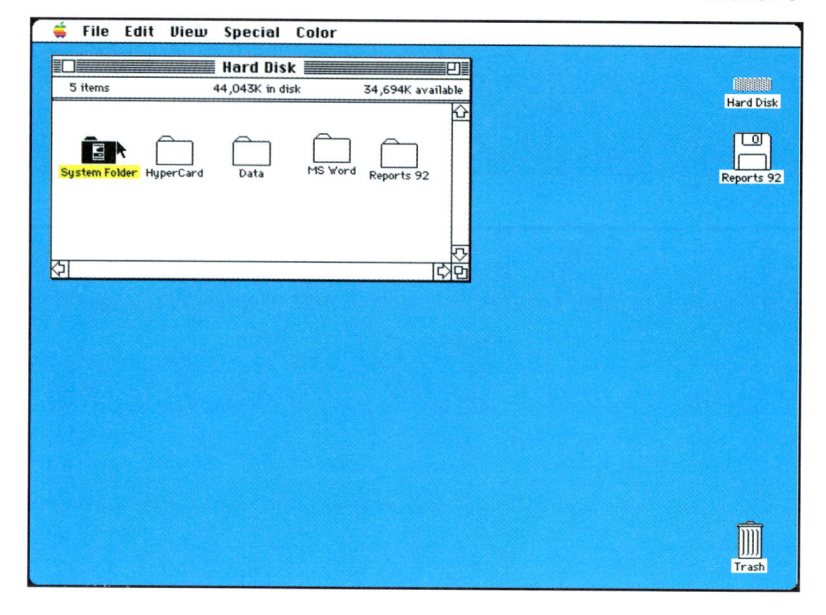

before

Oops!
Follow this same procedure to move the icon back to its original location.

1. Double-click on the **Hard Disk icon**.

   This step opens the Hard Disk window. If the window is already open, skip this step. Your hard disk might be named differently; double-click on the icon for your hard disk.

2. Click on the **System Folder** icon and hold down the mouse button.

   This step selects the icon. The icon darkens.

3. Drag the icon down.

   This step moves the icon in the window. As you drag, you see an outline of the icon move on-screen.

4. Release the mouse button.

   This step completes the move. The icon appears in its new location.

after

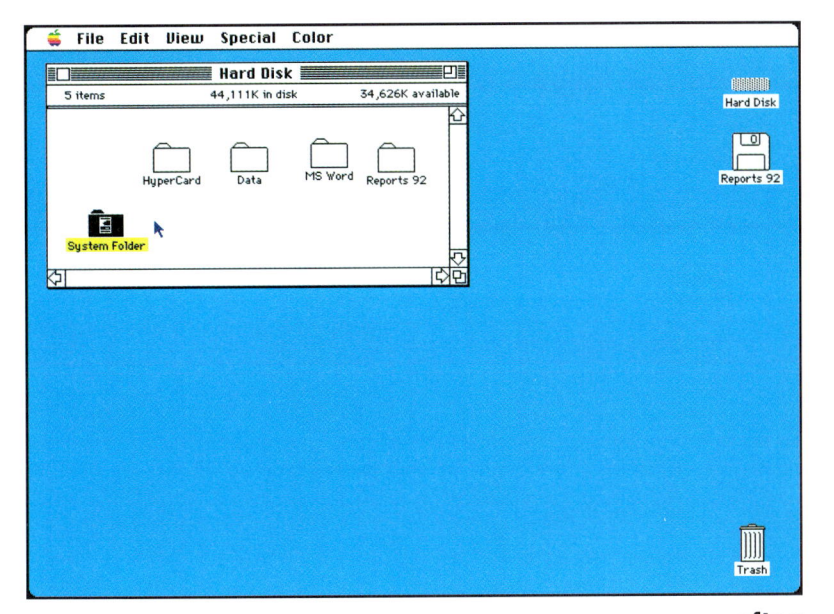

The names will not move?
You can only move icons. If the window is displayed in name view, you cannot rearrange the names. See TASK: *View a window by name* for information.

REVIEW

To move an icon

1. Click on the icon that you want to move; hold down the mouse button.

2. Drag the icon to the new location.

3. Release the mouse button.

TASK

Arrange icons

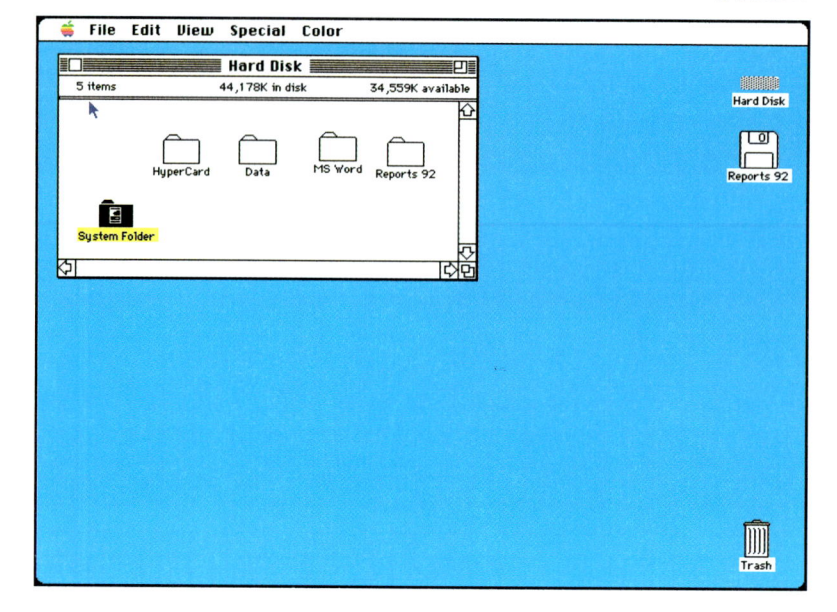

before

Oops!
You can arrange icons only if you are viewing a window in icon view.

1. **Double-click on the Hard Disk icon.**

   This step opens the Hard Disk window. If the window is already open, skip this step. Your hard disk might be named differently; double-click on the icon for your hard disk.

2. **Click on the System Folder icon and hold down the mouse button.**

   This step selects the System Folder icon. The icon darkens. The Before figure shows this step.

3. **Drag the icon down.**

   This step moves the icon in the window.

4. **Release the mouse button.**

   This step completes the move. The icon appears in its new location.

5. **Click on a blank part of the window.**

   The step deselects the icon and selects the window. To clean up the entire window, you must select the window. (If you have just one item selected, the following steps will align only that item.)

after

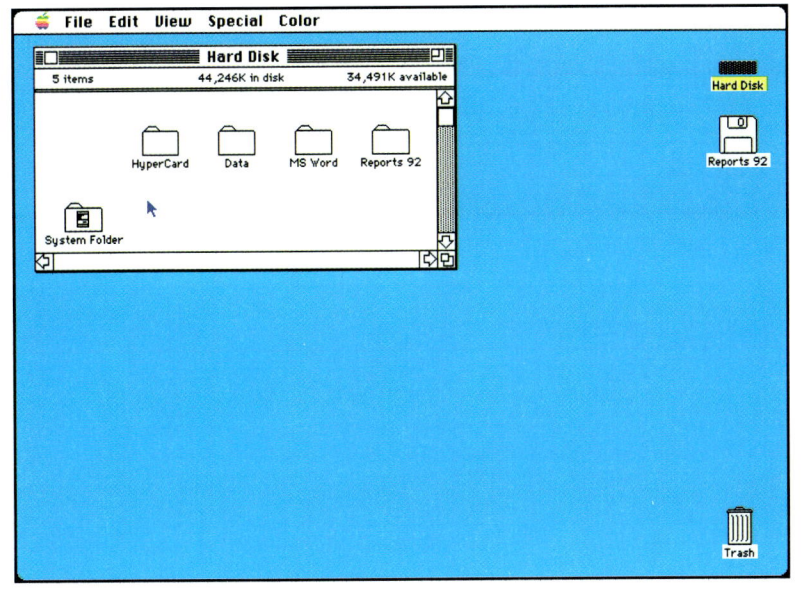

6. Click on **Special** in the menu bar; hold down the mouse button.

   This step opens the Special menu. You see a list of Special commands.

7. Drag down until you highlight **Clean Up Window**.

   This step selects the Clean Up Window command.

8. Release the mouse button.

   The icons are aligned to an invisible grid in the window (in no particular order). Some names might overlap in icon view. You can change the names (see *TASK: Rename a folder*) or change the view (see the tasks on viewing windows later in this section).

REVIEW

From the **Special** menu, select **Clean Up Window**.

To arrange icons

Viewing the Desktop

75

TASK

Open a folder

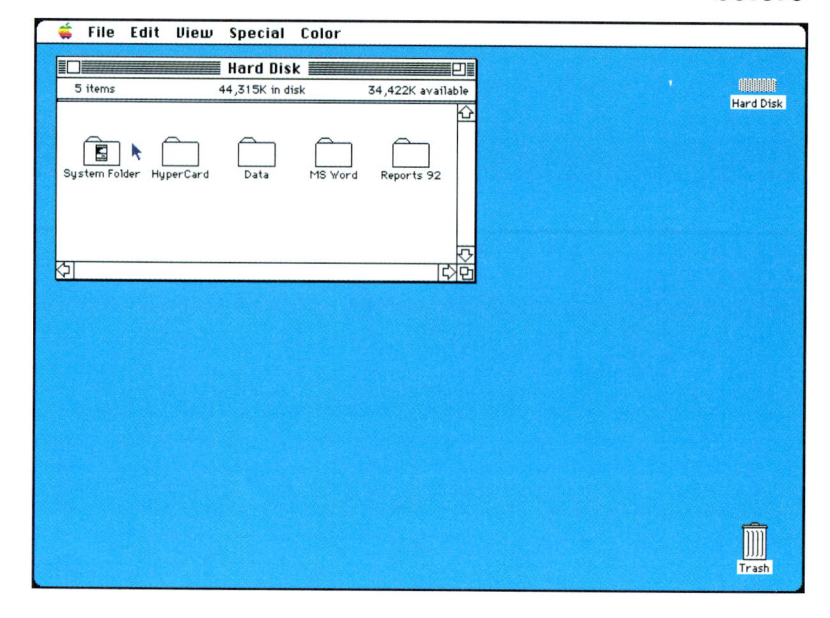

before

Oops!
To close the window, see
TASK: Close a window.

1. Double-click on the **Hard Disk** icon.

   This step opens the Hard Disk window. If the window is already open, skip this step. Your hard disk might be named differently; double-click on the icon for your hard disk.

2. Point to the **System Folder** icon.

   This is the folder that you want to open. In icon view, this folder contains a small picture of the Macintosh.

3. Double-click the mouse button.

   This step opens a folder window that displays the contents of the folder. The name of the folder, System Folder, appears in the title bar of the window.

   The default view lists files by name. You also can display icons rather than names, and you can change the order of the names. See later tasks in this section. (If you have modified the view, you will see the modified view rather than a name view.) If you look at the folder in icon view, the number of items, the disk space taken by the contents, and the disk space remaining appear under the title bar.

   Note that all disk and folder windows look identical. They are called disk window and folder window here to distinguish the contents of the window.

76

Easy **Macintosh**

after

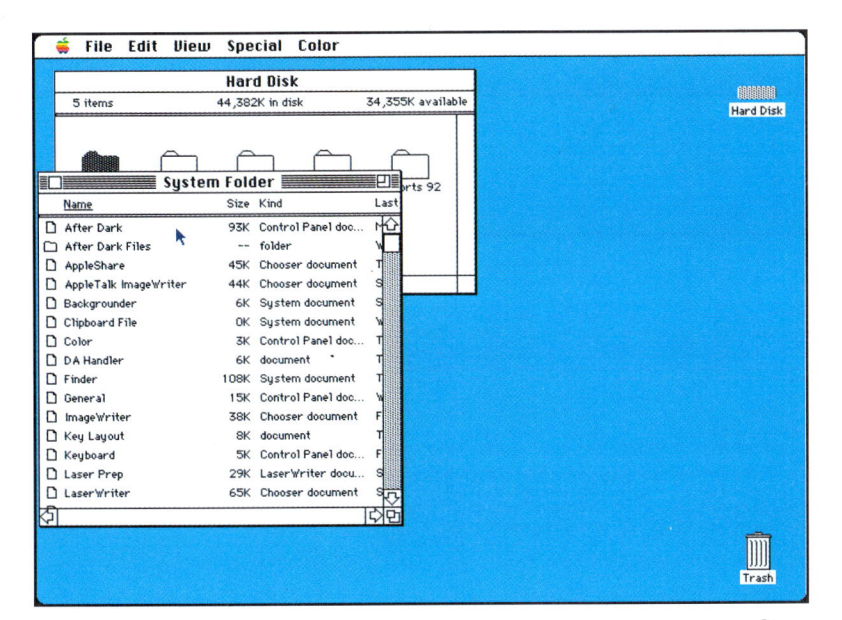

Arrange windows
You can move and resize this window. See *TASK: Move a window* and *TASK: Resize a window*.

REVIEW

Double-click on the **folder icon**.

To open a folder

Viewing the Desktop

77

TASK

Select a window

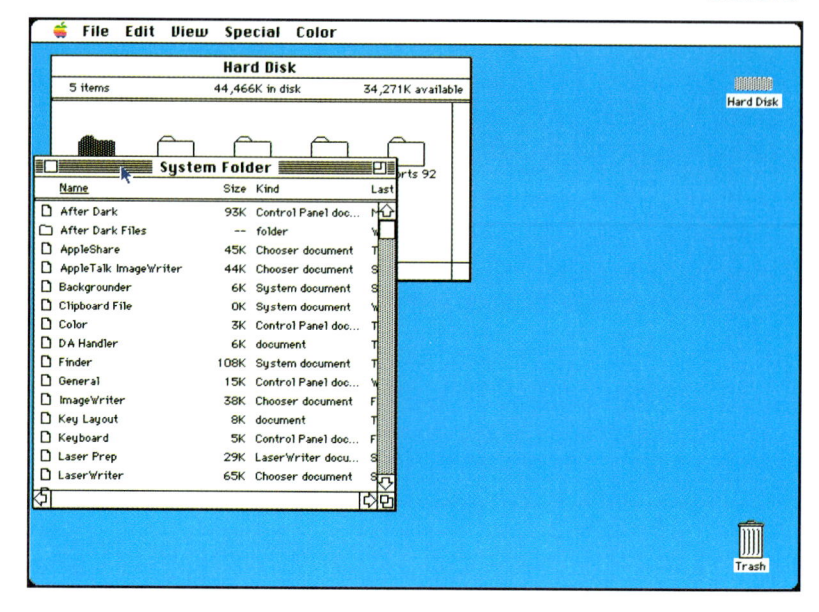

before

Oops!
Follow this procedure to select a different window.

1. Double-click on the **Hard Disk** icon.

   This step opens the Hard Disk window. If the window is already open, skip this step. Your hard disk might be named differently; double-click on the icon for your hard disk.

2. Double-click on the **System Folder** icon.

   This step opens the System Folder window. You see the contents of this folder on-screen. Two windows are now open. The active window (System Folder) includes lines in the title bar. You should also be able to see the Hard Disk window. This title bar does not have lines—it is inactive. (If you cannot see the hard disk window, move or resize the System Folder window.)

3. Click any place on the **Hard Disk** window.

   This step moves the hard disk window to the top of the stack. The System Folder window is still open, but it is not active.

78

Easy Macintosh

after

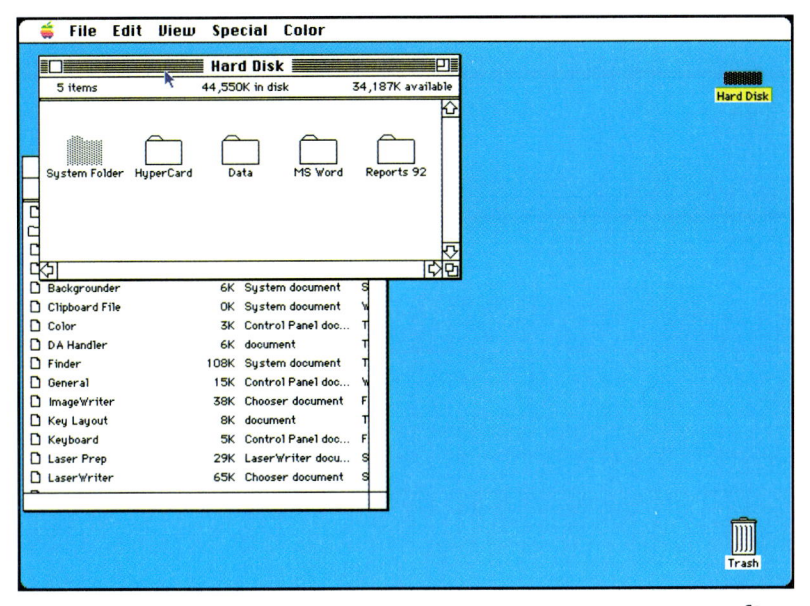

REVIEW

Click on the window you want to select.

To select a window

Viewing the Desktop

79

TASK

Scroll a window

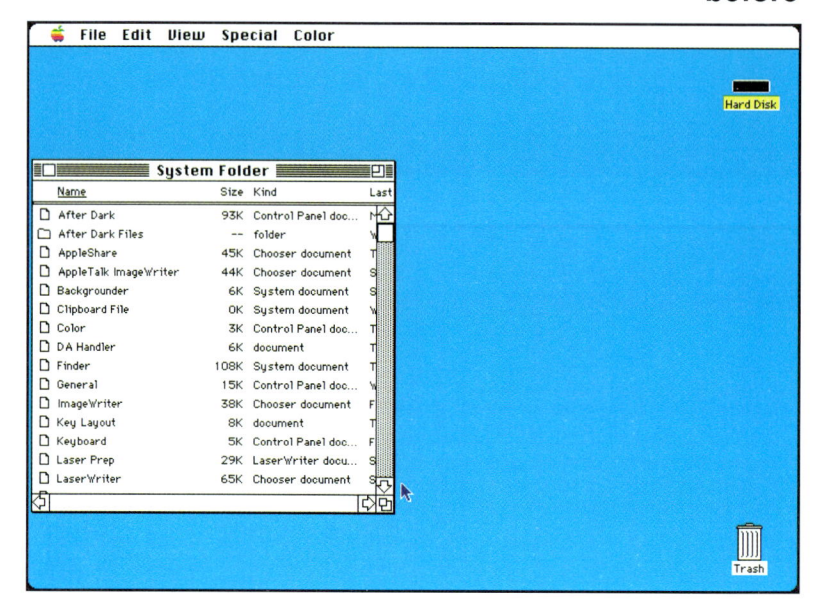

before

Oops!
Click on the up scroll arrow to scroll back up.

1. Double-click on the **Hard Disk** icon.

   This step opens the hard disk window. If the window is already open, skip this step. Your hard disk might be named differently; double-click on the icon for your hard disk.

2. Double-click on the **System Folder** icon.

   This step opens the System Folder window. You see the contents of this folder on-screen. This window contains more items than can be displayed in the current window. Along the side of the window, you see the scroll bar (gray area), scroll arrows (arrows at top and bottom of scroll bar), and scroll box (white box within scroll bar).

3. Click twice on the **down scroll arrow**.

   This step displays approximately two more lines in the folder window. Note that the scroll box has moved down to show where you are in the overall screen.

80

Easy **Macintosh**

after

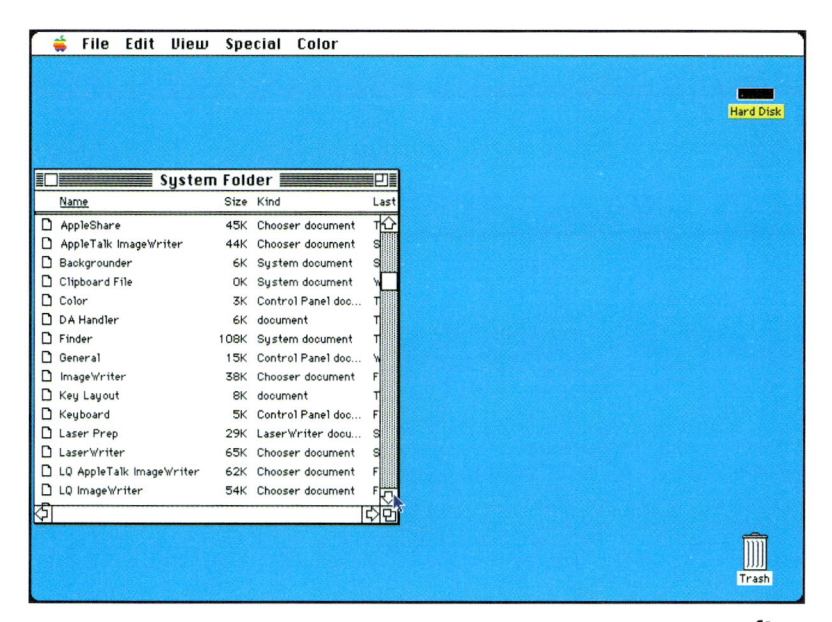

Click on the **scroll arrows** or drag the **scroll box**.

Scroll the window another way
You also can click on the scroll box, hold down the mouse button, and drag the scroll box to display other parts of the window. The scroll box indicates the relative position of the current window view.

REVIEW

To scroll a window

Scroll bar white?
If the scroll bar is white, the entire contents of the window are displayed. You cannot scroll this window.

TASK

View a window by small icon

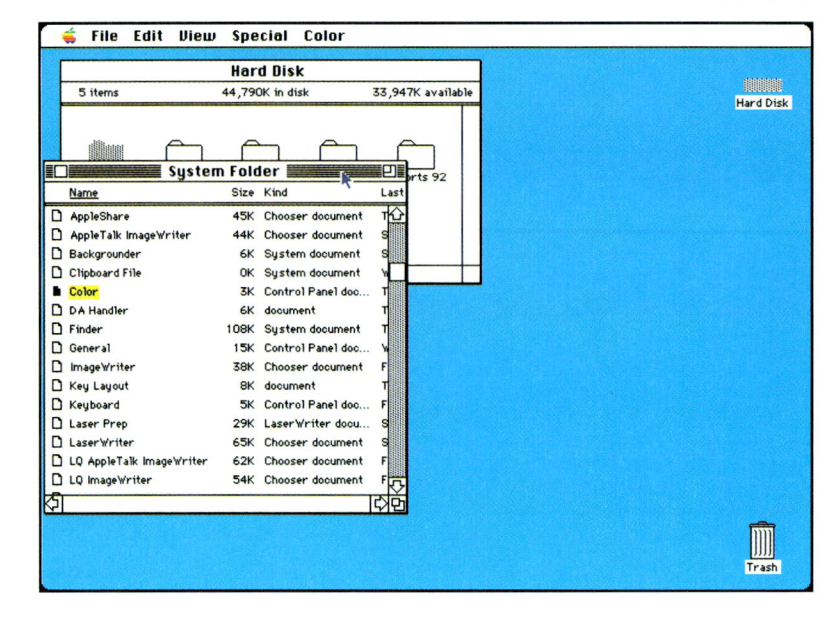

before

Oops!
To return to regular icon view, select by Icon from the View menu.

1. Double-click on the **Hard Disk** icon.

   This step opens the Hard Disk window. If the window is already open, skip this step. Your hard disk might be named differently; double-click on the icon for your hard disk.

2. Double-click on the **System Folder** icon.

   This step opens the System Folder window. You see a list of the contents of this folder. By default, the contents are listed by name. (If this window is already open, skip this step.)

3. Click on **View** in the menu bar; hold down the mouse button.

   This step opens the View menu. You see a list of View commands.

4. Drag down until you highlight **by Small Icon**.

   This step selects the by Small Icon command.

5. Release the mouse button.

   Small icons appear—in no particular order—for each of the items in the folder. The names of some of the icons might overlap; also, the window is probably too small to display all the icons. Scroll the window to see the other icons (see *TASK: Scroll a window*).

   You can resize the window to see all the icons.

Easy **Macintosh**

after

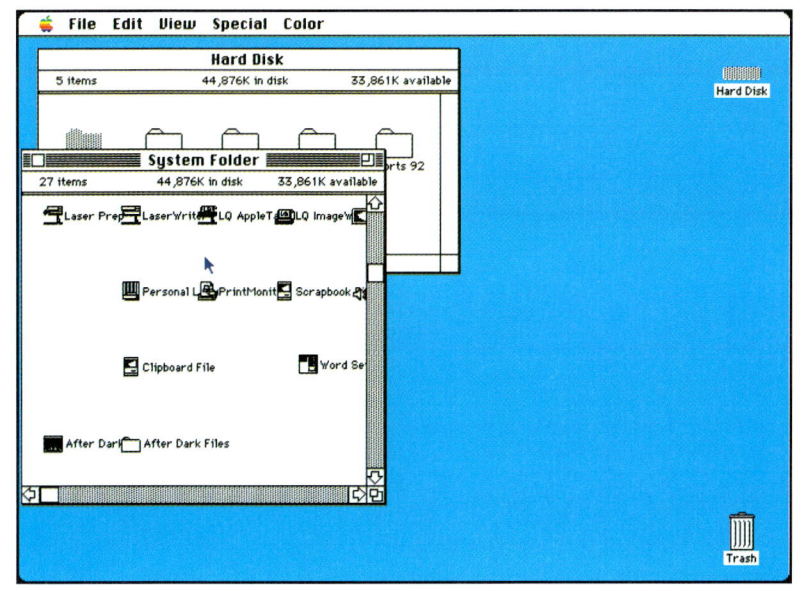

Which view appears?
Keep in mind that the Macintosh remembers how you last viewed the window. This view will be used the next time you open the window. Also, you can view each window differently—changing the view for window does not change the view for all windows.

REVIEW

To view a window by small icon

1. Open the window.
2. From the **View** menu, select **by Small Icon**.

Viewing the Desktop

83

TASK

View a window by name

before

Oops!
To restore the original view, select the view that you want from the View menu.

1. Double-click on the **Hard Disk** icon.

   This step opens the Hard Disk window. If the window is already open, skip this step. Your hard disk might be named differently; double-click on the icon for your hard disk.

2. Double-click on the **System Folder** icon.

   This step opens the System Folder window. You see the contents of the folder. If you followed the preceding task, the contents appear by small icon. If you didn't follow this task, you might see a different view.

3. Click on **View** in the menu bar; hold down the mouse button.

   This step opens the View menu. You see a list of View commands.

4. Drag down until you highlighted **by Name**.

   This step selects the by Name command.

5. Release the mouse button.

   The name of each item—as well as the size, kind, and modification dates—appear in the window. The names are listed in alphabetical order. Note that Name is underlined in the window. This underline reminds you how the window is sorted.

   You might need to resize the window to show all the columns.

Easy **Macintosh**

after

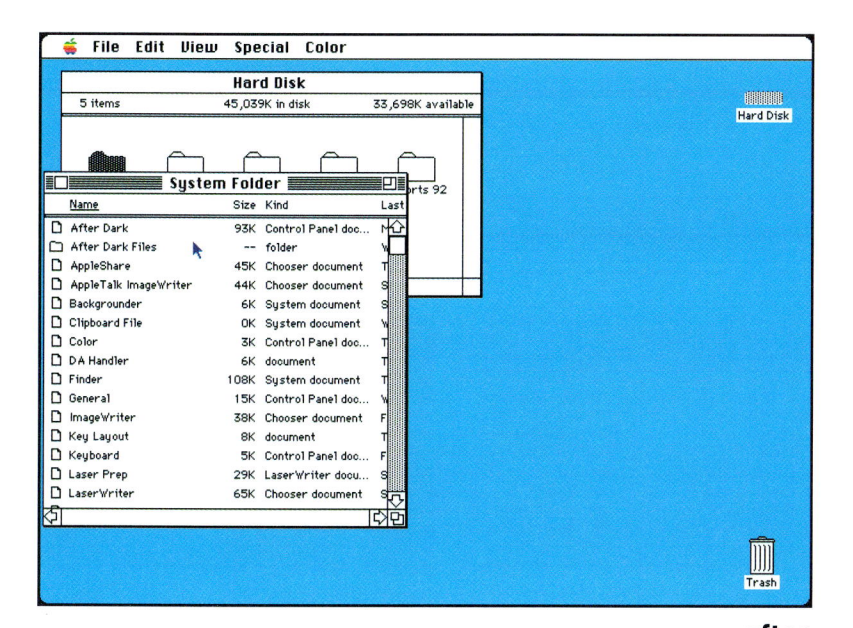

Which view appears?
Keep in mind that the Macintosh remembers how you last viewed the window. This view will be used the next time you open the window.

REVIEW

1. Open the window.
2. From the **View** menu, select **by Name**.

To view a window by name

Viewing the Desktop

85

TASK

View a window by date

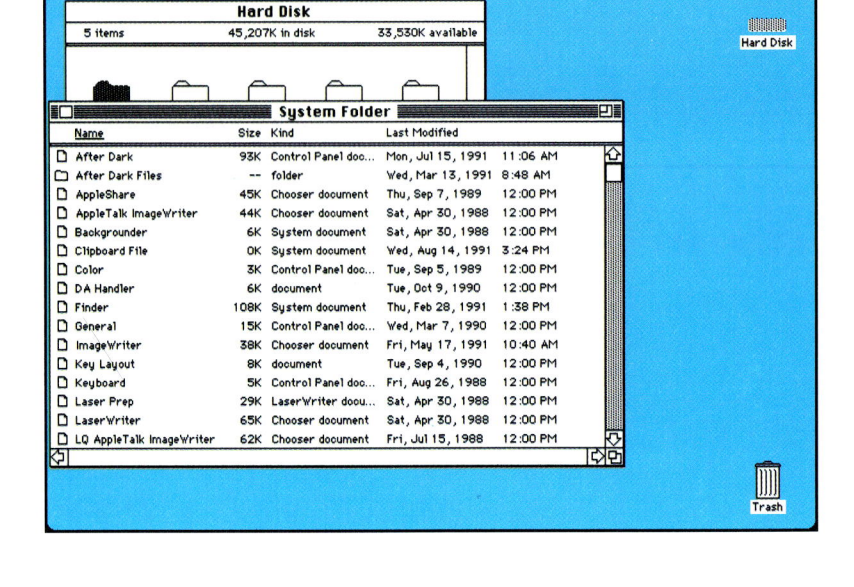

before

Oops!
To restore the original view, select the view that you want from the View menu.

1. **Double-click on the Hard Disk icon.**

   This step opens the Hard Disk window. If the window is already open, skip this step. Your hard disk might be named differently; double-click on the icon for your hard disk.

2. **Double-click on the System Folder icon.**

   This step opens the System Folder window. You see the contents of the folder. If you followed the preceding task, the contents appear by name. If you didn't follow this task, you might see a different view. You might need to resize the window to show all the columns.

3. **Click on View in the menu bar; hold down the mouse button.**

   This step opens the View menu. You see a list of View commands.

4. **Drag down until you highlight by Date.**

   This step selects the by Date command.

5. **Release the mouse button.**

   The items are listed by name and sorted by date (beginning with the most recently modified items). Note that `Last Modified` is underlined in the window. This underline reminds you how the window is sorted.

after

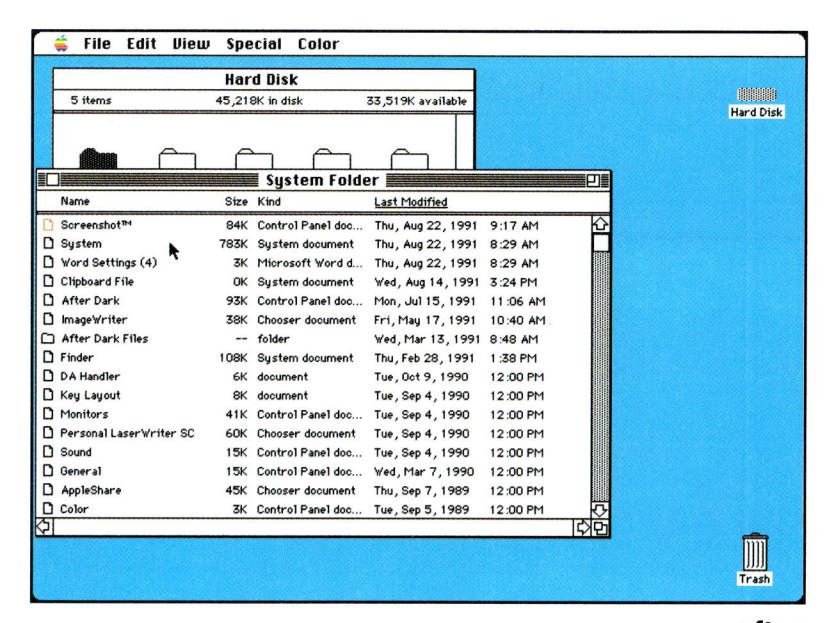

Which view appears?
Keep in mind that the Macintosh remembers how you last viewed the window. This view will be used the next time you open the window.

REVIEW

1. Open the window.
2. From the **View** menu, select **by Date**.

To view a window by date

Viewing the Desktop

87

TASK

View a window by size

before

Oops!
To restore the original view, select the view that you want from the View menu.

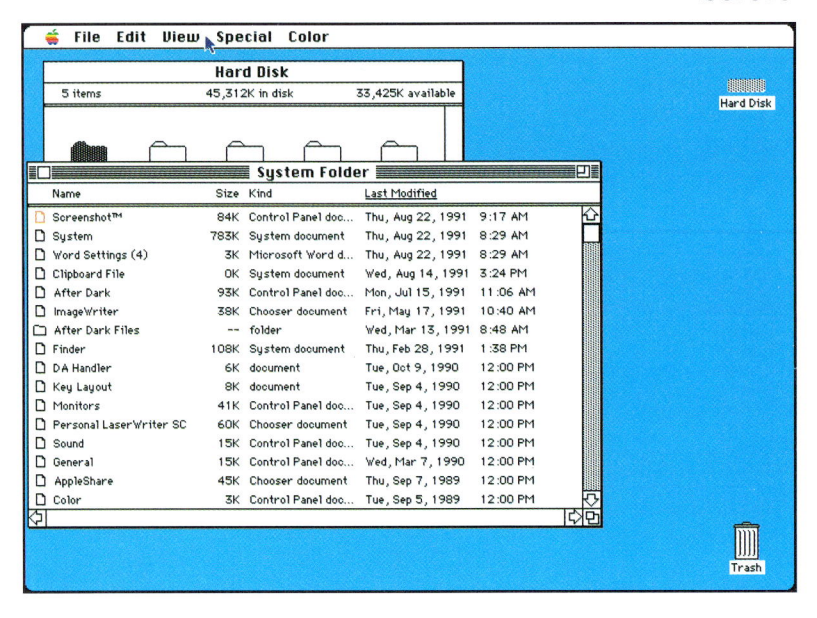

1. **Double-click on the Hard Disk icon.**

   This step opens the Hard Disk window. If the window is already open, skip this step. Your hard disk might be named differently; double-click on the icon for your hard disk.

2. **Double-click on the System Folder icon.**

   This step opens the System Folder window. You see a list of the contents of this folder.

3. **Click on View in the menu bar; hold down the mouse button.**

   This step opens the View menu. You see a list of View commands.

4. **Drag down until you highlight by Size.**

   This step selects the by Size command.

5. **Release the mouse button.**

   The items are listed by name and sorted by size (biggest to smallest). Note that Size is underlined in the window. This underline reminds you how the window is sorted.

Easy **Macintosh**

after

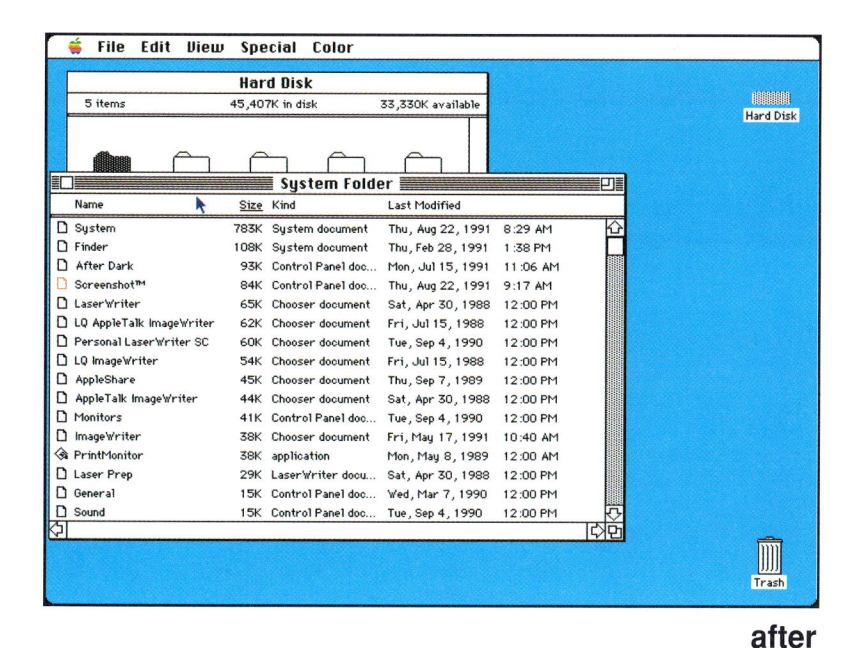

Which view appears?
Keep in mind that the Macintosh remembers how you last viewed the window. This view will be used the next time you open the window.

REVIEW

1. Open the window.
2. From the **View** menu, select **by Size**.

To view a window by size

Try this tip
When you need to clean up your hard disk—free up memory—use this view to see which folders and documents are taking up the most memory.

Viewing the Desktop

TASK

View a window by kind

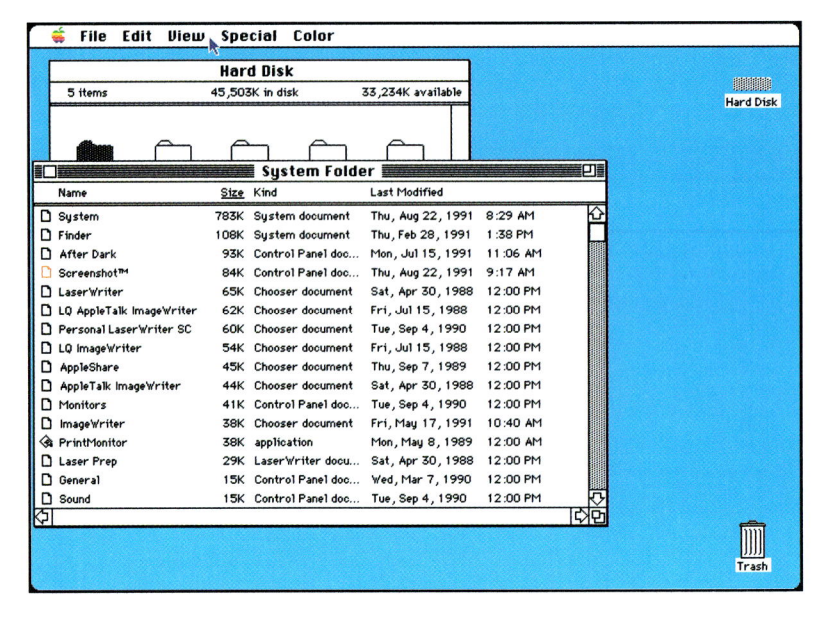

before

Oops!
To restore the original view, select the view that you want from the View menu.

1. **Double-click on the Hard Disk icon.**
   This step opens the Hard Disk window. If the window is already open, skip this step. Your hard disk might be named differently; double-click on the icon for your hard disk.

2. **Double-click on the System Folder icon.**
   This step opens the System Folder window. You see a list of the contents of this folder.

3. **Click on View in the menu bar; hold down the mouse button.**
   This step opens the View menu. You see a list of View commands.

4. **Drag down until you highlight by Kind.**
   This step selects the by Kind command.

5. **Release the mouse button.**
   The items are listed by name and sorted by kind (such as Application, Chooser, and Control Panel). Note that Kind is underlined in the window. This underline reminds you how the window is sorted.

Easy **Macintosh**

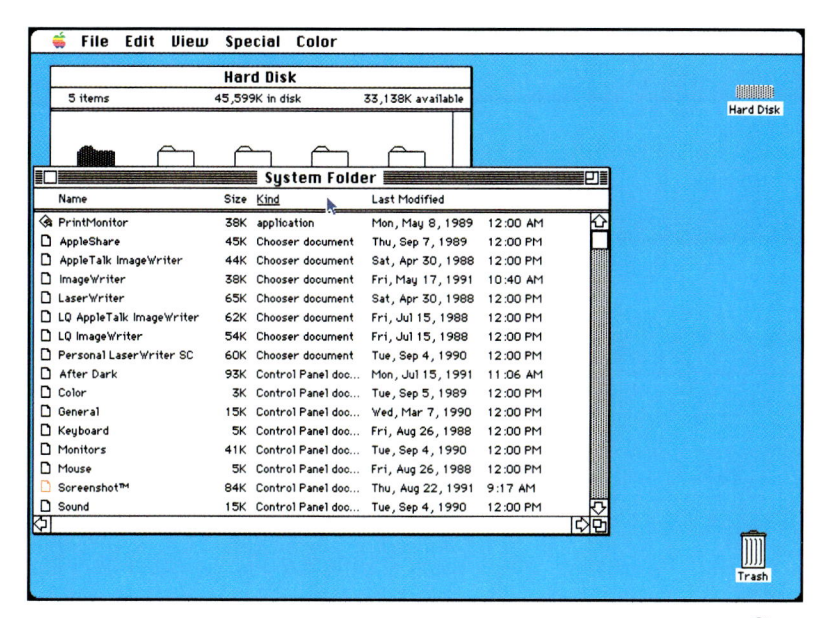

after

1. Open the window.
2. From the **View** menu, select **by Kind**.

Which view appears?
Keep in mind that the Macintosh remembers how you last viewed the window. This view will be used the next time you open the window.

REVIEW

To view a window by kind

Viewing the Desktop

Working with Folders

This section covers the following tasks:

Create a new folder

Rename a folder

Display information about a folder

Copy a folder

Delete a folder

Retrieve an item from the Trash

Empty the Trash

TASK

Create a new folder

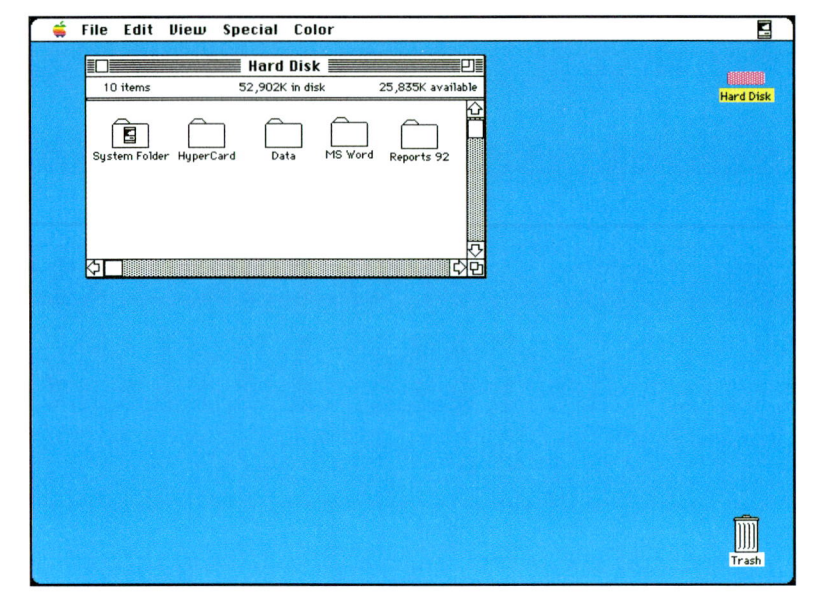

before

Oops!
To delete the folder, see *TASK: Delete a folder*.

1. **Double-click on the Hard Disk icon.**

   This step opens the Hard Disk window. If the window is already open, skip this step. Your hard disk might be named differently; double-click on the icon for your hard disk.

   The new folder will be placed on the hard disk.

2. **Click on File in the menu bar; hold down the mouse button.**

   This step opens the File menu. You see a list of File commands.

3. **Drag down until you highlight New Folder.**

   This step selects the New Folder command.

4. **Release the mouse button.**

   A folder icon is placed in the hard disk window. The folder is named Empty Folder and is selected.

5. **Type Proposals.**

   This is the name of the folder. The name may be up to 31 characters long; do not include a colon (:) in the name.

6. **Press Return.**

   Pressing Return confirms the name.

Easy **Macintosh**

after

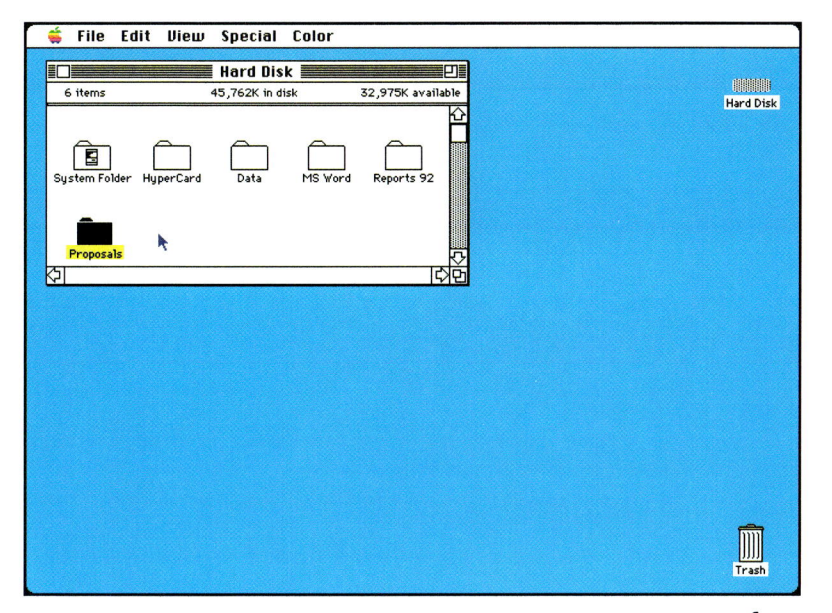

Try a shortcut
To select the New Folder command, press the ⌘-N keyboard shortcut.

REVIEW

1. Open the window in which you want to place the new folder.
2. From the **File** menu, select **New Folder**.
3. Type a folder name.
4. Press **Return**.

To create a new folder

Create nesting folders
You also can place folders within folders (called *nesting folders*). To do so, open the folder you want to contain the new folder (see *TASK: Open a folder*). Then create the new folder.

Working with Folders

TASK

Rename a folder

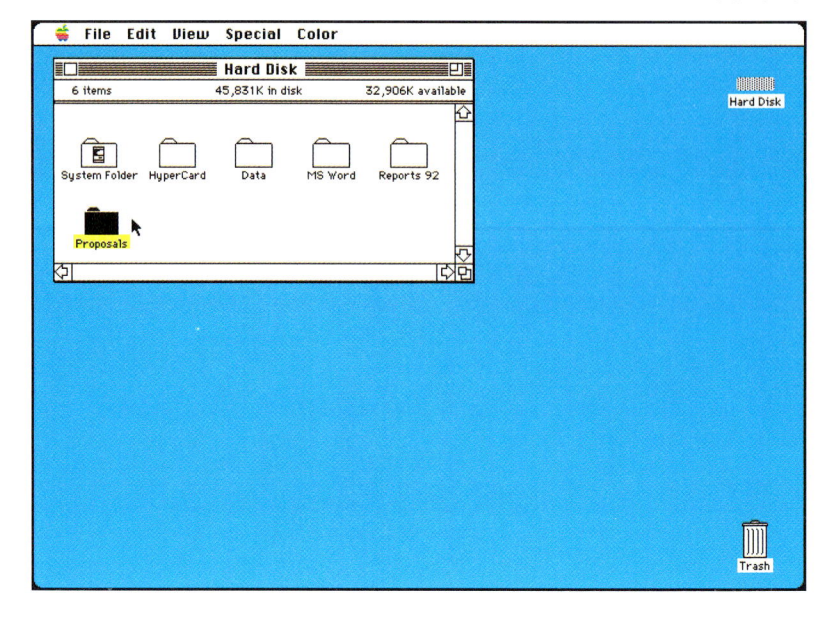

before

Oops!
Follow this to procedure again to rename the folder.

1. Double-click on the **Hard Disk** icon.

   This step opens the Hard Disk window. If the window is already open, skip this step. Your hard disk might be named differently; double-click on the icon for your hard disk.

2. Click on the **Proposals** icon.

   This step selects the icon; it should be highlighted on-screen.

3. Type **Book Proposals**.

   This is the new name for the folder. If you make a mistake while typing, press the Delete key to delete the error.

4. Press **Return**.

   Pressing Return confirms the new name.

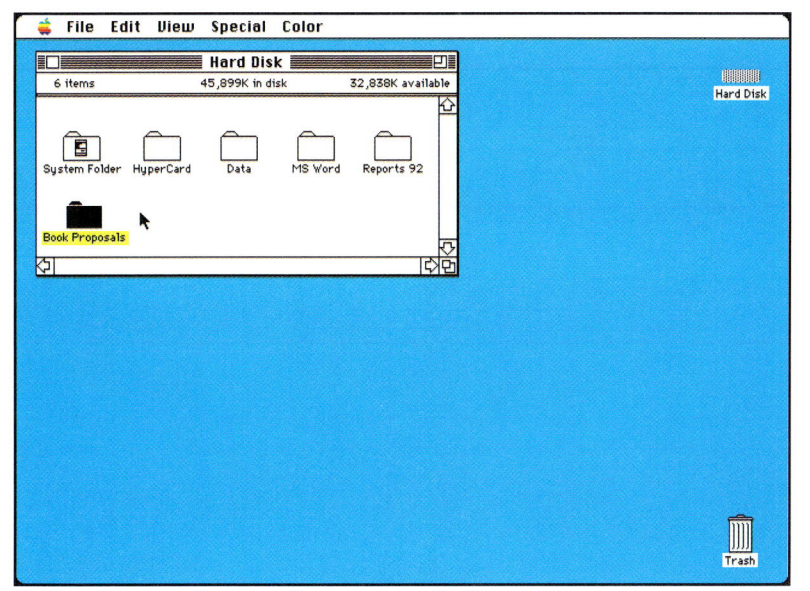

after

1. Click on the **icon** you want to rename.
2. Type the new name.
3. Press **Return**.

Use a different method
You also can rename a folder by highlighting the folder and moving the mouse over the name. The pointer becomes a cursor. Click to insert the pointer where you want to make the change.

REVIEW

To rename a folder

TASK

Display information about a folder

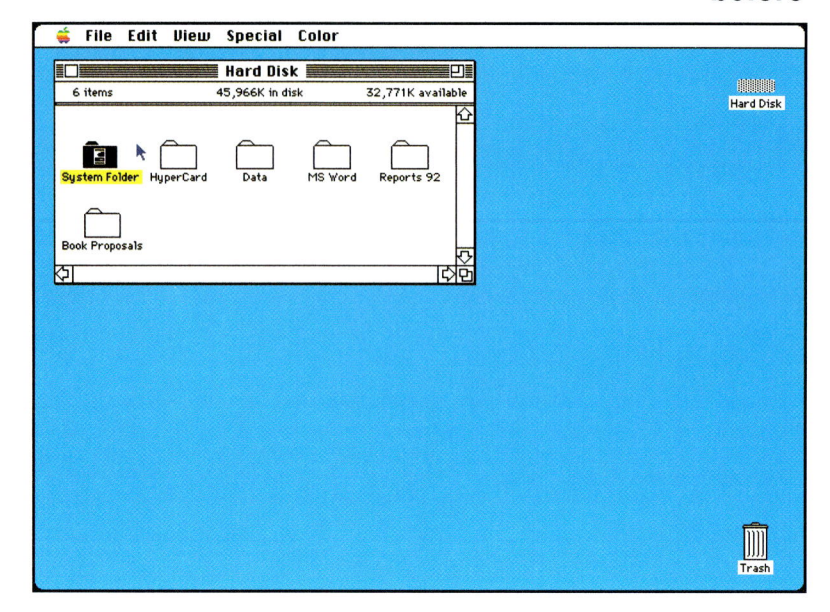

before

Oops!
Click on the close box to close the window.

1. Double-click on the **Hard Disk** icon.

   This step opens the Hard Disk window. If the window is already open, skip this step. Your hard disk might be named differently; double-click on the icon for your hard disk.

2. Click on the **System Folder** icon.

   This step selects the System Folder. (If you want to open the folder, double-click on the icon.)

3. Click on **File** in the menu bar; hold down the mouse button.

   This step opens the File menu. You see a list of File commands.

4. Drag down until you highlight **Get Info**.

   This step selects the Get Info command.

5. Release the mouse button.

   You see an Info window that displays information about the selected item:

Kind	Kind of selected item, in this case, a folder.
Size	Size in bytes and kilobytes (K) and the number of files in the folder.

Easy **Macintosh**

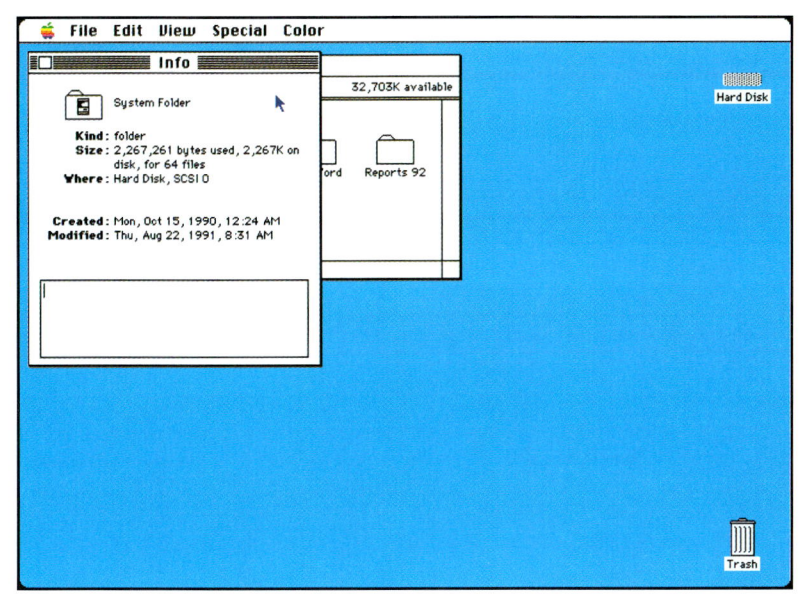

after

Where	Location of selected item; in this case, on the hard disk.
Created	Date that the folder was created.
Modified	Date that the folder was last modified.

The insertion point is in a comments box at the bottom of the window. If you want, you can type a comment. You might, for instance, make a note of what the folder contains.

6. Click on the **close box**.
   This step closes the Info window.

Try a shortcut
Select the folder and then press the ⌘-I keyboard shortcut to select the Get Info command.

REVIEW

1. Click on the **folder** for which you want information.
2. From the **File** menu, select **Get Info**.
3. Click on the **close box**.

To display information about a folder

Working with Folders

99

TASK

Copy a folder

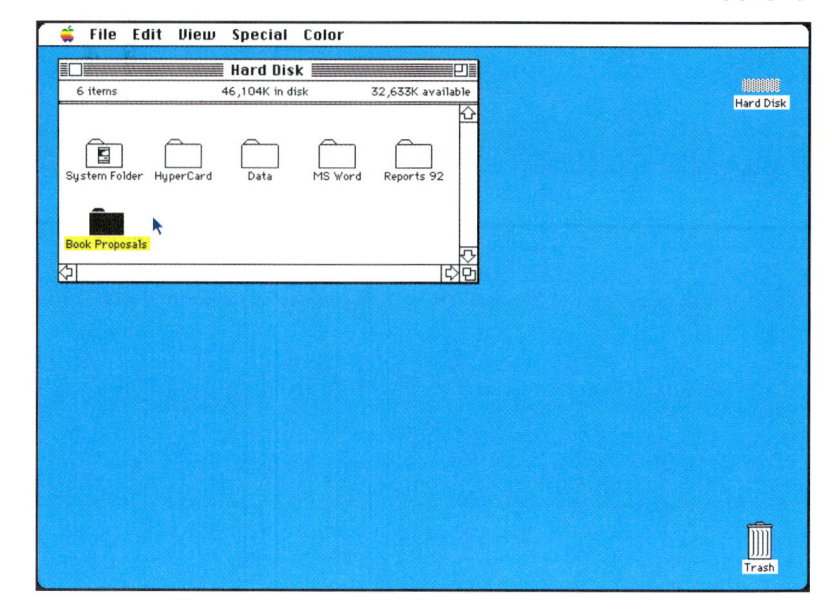

before

Oops!
If you don't want the copy, delete it. See *TASK: Delete a folder*.

1. Double-click on the **Hard Disk** icon.

    This step opens the Hard Disk window. If the window is already open, skip this step. Your hard disk might be named differently; double-click on the icon for your hard disk.

2. Click on the **Book Proposals** icon.

    This step selects the Book Proposals folder. If you don't have this folder, click on one that you do have. (Be sure not to select the System Folder, however. This folder is special, and having two copies of it will confuse the Macintosh.)

3. Click on **File** in the menu bar; hold down the mouse button.

    This step opens the File menu. You see a list of File commands.

4. Drag down until you highlight **Duplicate**.

    This step selects the Duplicate command.

5. Release the mouse button.

    You see a progress window as the folder and its contents are copied. The copy of the folder is placed in the window and is named *Copy of Book Proposals*.

Easy **Macintosh**

after

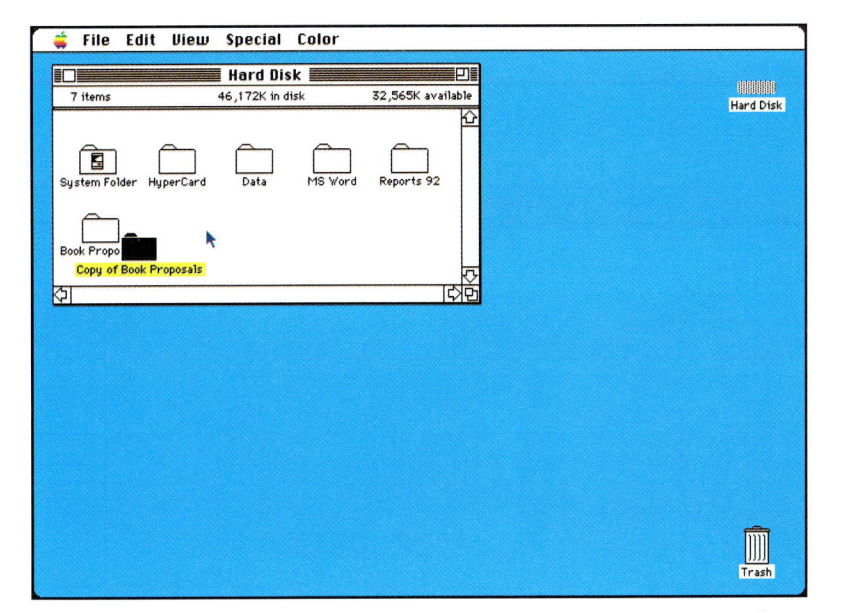

Open the folder
To open the folder, double-click on the folder icon.

REVIEW

1. Click on the **folder** that you want to copy.
2. From the **File** menu, select **Duplicate**.

To copy a folder

Try a shortcut
Select the file or folder and press the ⌘-D keyboard shortcut to select the Duplicate command.

Working with Folders

101

TASK

Delete a folder

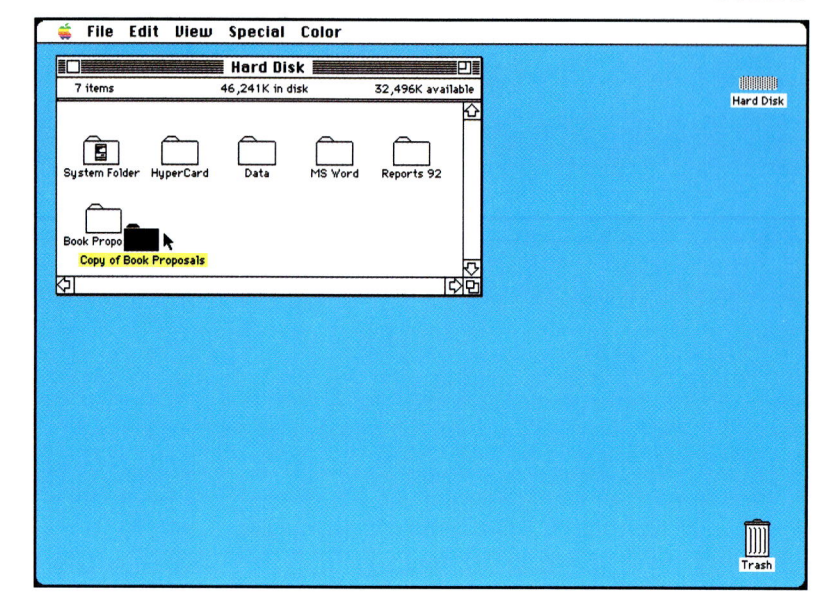

before

Oops!
If the Trash has not been emptied (see *TASK: Empty the Trash*), you can retrieve the folder. See *TASK: Retrieve an item from the Trash can icon.*

1. **Double-click on the Hard Disk icon.**

   This step opens the Hard Disk window. If the window is already open, skip this step. Your hard disk might be named differently; double-click on the icon for your hard disk.

2. **Click on the Copy of Book Proposal icon.**

   This step selects the Copy of Book Proposal folder. If you don't have a copy of this folder, see *TASK: Copy a folder* to create the folder or click on a folder that you do have. Be sure to select one that you don't need. Do not click on the System Folder.

3. **Hold down the mouse button and drag the folder icon to the Trash can icon.**

   This step places the folder and its contents into the Trash. The Trash can icon darkens and expands.

4. **Release the mouse button.**

   This step completes the deletion. When the Trash contains an item, the sides of the Trash can icon bulge.

Easy **Macintosh**

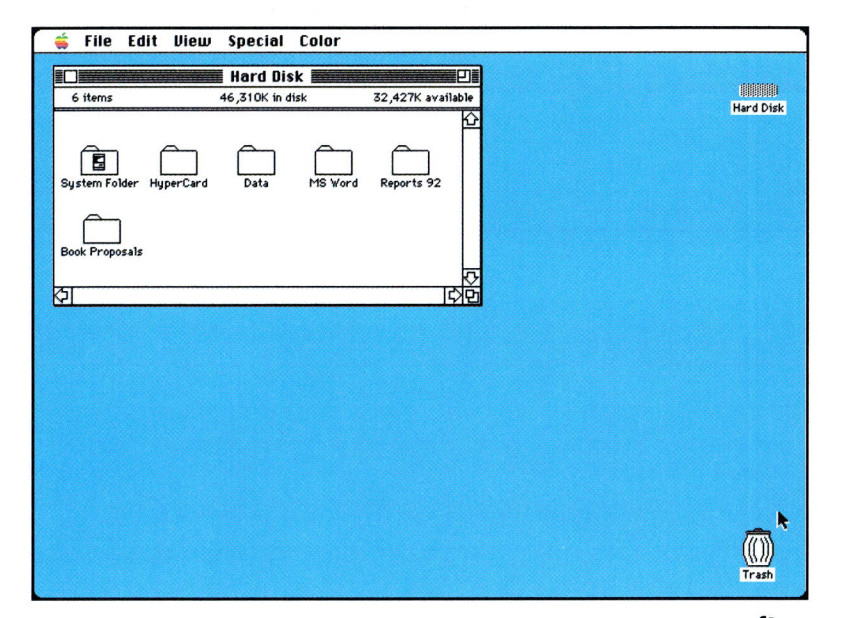

after

1. Point to the folder that you want to delete.
2. Click and hold the mouse button.
3. Drag the folder icon to the **Trash can** icon.
4. Release the mouse button.

Working with Folders

REVIEW

To delete a folder

Be careful!
Keep in mind that you are deleting the folder and all its contents. Be sure that you don't delete something you need. Never delete the System Folder.

Delete an application
If you delete a folder that contains an application, an alert message will appear. You must confirm that you want to delete the application. Chances are, you will not want to delete the application.

TASK

Retrieve an item from the Trash

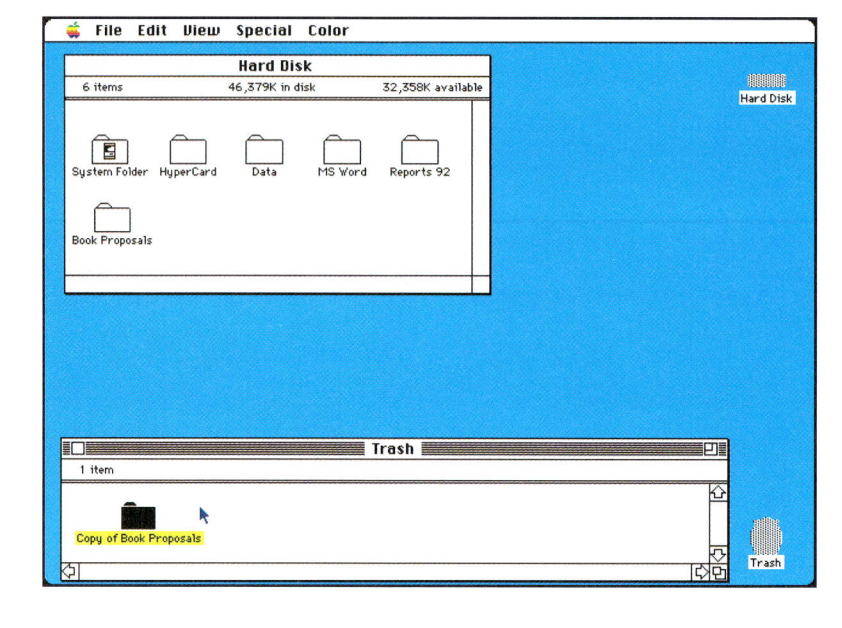

before

Oops!
To remove an item permanently from the Trash (delete the item), you must empty the Trash. See *TASK: Empty the Trash*.

1. Double-click on the **Trash can icon**.
   This step opens the Trash can icon and displays all the documents and folders that are still in the Trash. The title bar displays the name of the window, Trash. The items in the Trash appear in the window, below the title bar.

   If the Trash is empty, delete something first. See *TASK: Delete a folder*.

2. Point to the **Copy of Book Proposals** icon.
   This step selects the Copy of Book Proposals folder, which is is the folder you want to retrieve.

3. Click and hold down the mouse button.
   This step selects the folder icon.

4. Drag the icon back to the hard disk window.
   This step moves the icon from the Trash to the hard disk.

5. Release the mouse button.
   This step restores the deleted item.

6. In the Trash window, click on the **close box**.
   This step closes the Trash window. The close box is the small box in the upper left corner of the Trash window.

Easy **Macintosh**

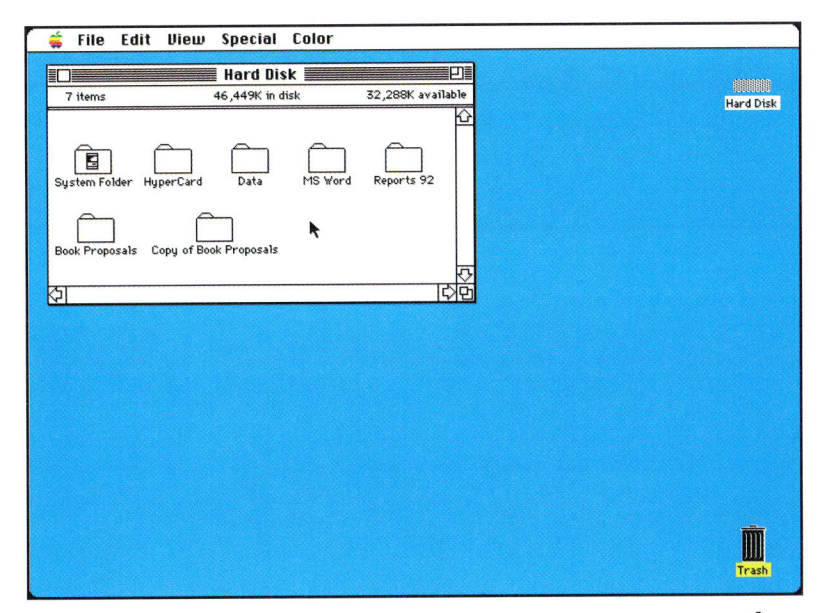

after

1. Double-click on the **Trash can** icon.

2. Click on the **item** you want to retrieve; hold down the mouse button.

3. Drag the item to the window where you want the item placed.

4. Release the mouse button.

Be careful!
If the Trash has been emptied, you cannot retrieve items. The Trash is emptied and the icons within it are deleted when an application program starts, when the Macintosh is shut down, when you choose the Empty Trash command from the Special menu, and when you eject a disk.

REVIEW

To retrieve an item from the Trash

Use a different method
You also can restore the deleted item by clicking on the item. Then select Put Away from the File menu.

Working with Folders

105

TASK

Empty the Trash

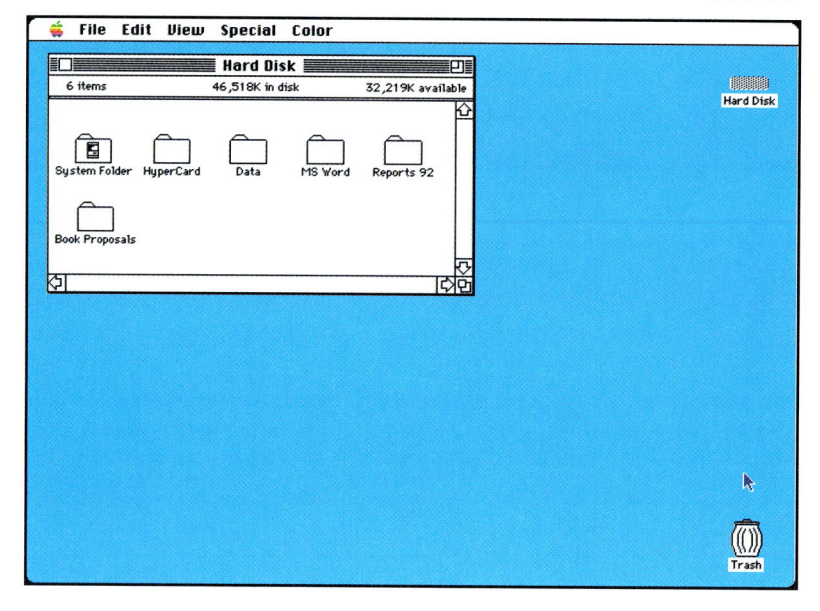

before

Oops!
Check the Trash before you empty it. After you empty it, you cannot retrieve any items.

1. Click on the **Copy of Book Proposals** icon and drag it to the **Trash can** icon.

   For more information on deleting a folder, see *TASK: Delete a folder*. When the Trash contains an item, it bulges (as in the Before screen).

2. Click on **Special** in the menu bar; hold down the mouse button.

   This step opens the Special menu. You see a list of Special commands.

3. Drag down until you highlight **Empty Trash**.

   This step selects the Empty Trash command. All the items in the Trash are deleted—you cannot retrieve them. When the Trash contains items, the sides of the Trash can icon bulge. When the Trash is emptied, the Trash can icon returns to its normal shape.

Easy **Macintosh**

after

From the **Special** menu, select **Empty Trash**.

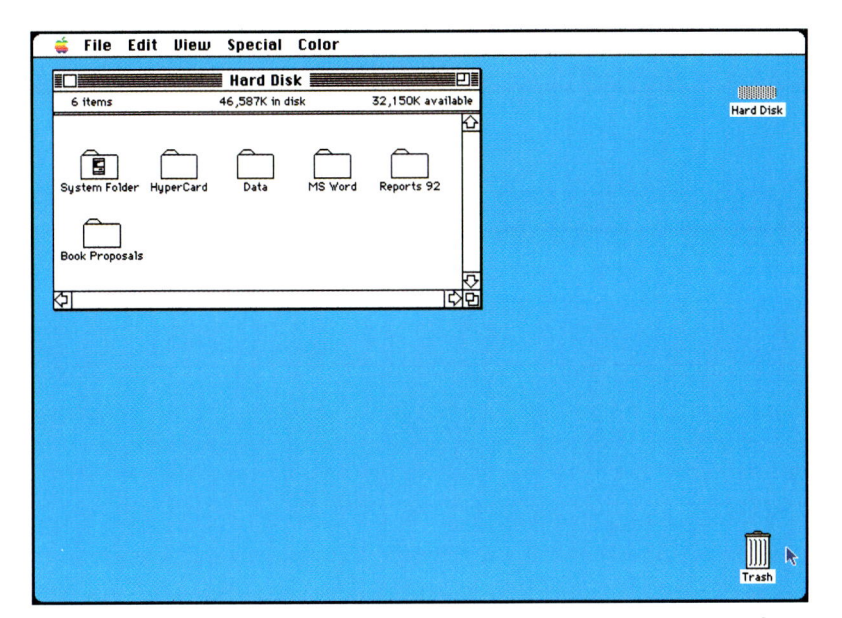

When does the Trash empty?
The Trash is also emptied when you start an application, shut down the Macintosh, or eject a disk.

REVIEW

To empty the Trash

Be Careful!
If you try to throw away an important item, such as an application, the Macintosh will warn you. You must confirm that you do indeed want to delete the item.

Working with Folders

Working with Documents and Applications

This section covers the following tasks:

Display information about a document

Lock a document

Duplicate a document

Rename a document

Move a document to another folder

Copy a document to another folder

Copy a document to another disk

Delete a document

Find a document

TASK

Display information about a document

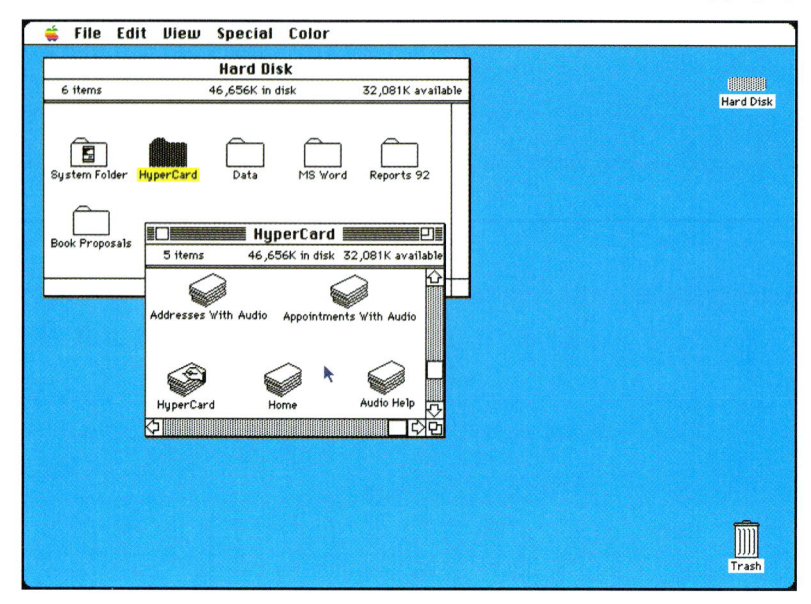

before

Oops!
Click on the close box to close the window.

1. Double-click on the **Hard Disk** icon.

   This step opens the Hard Disk window. If the window is already open, skip this step. Your hard disk might be named differently; double-click on the icon for your hard disk.

2. Double-click on the **HyperCard** icon.

   This step opens the HyperCard folder. You should have this folder. If not, open any folder.

3. Click on the **Home** icon.

   This step selects the Home document. Be sure to click on it only once; do not double-click on it.

4. Click on **File** in the menu bar; hold down the mouse button.

   This step opens the File menu. You see a list of File commands.

5. Drag down until you highlight **Get Info**.

   This step selects the Get Info command.

6. Release the mouse button.

   You see an Info window that displays information about the selected item:

110

Easy Macintosh

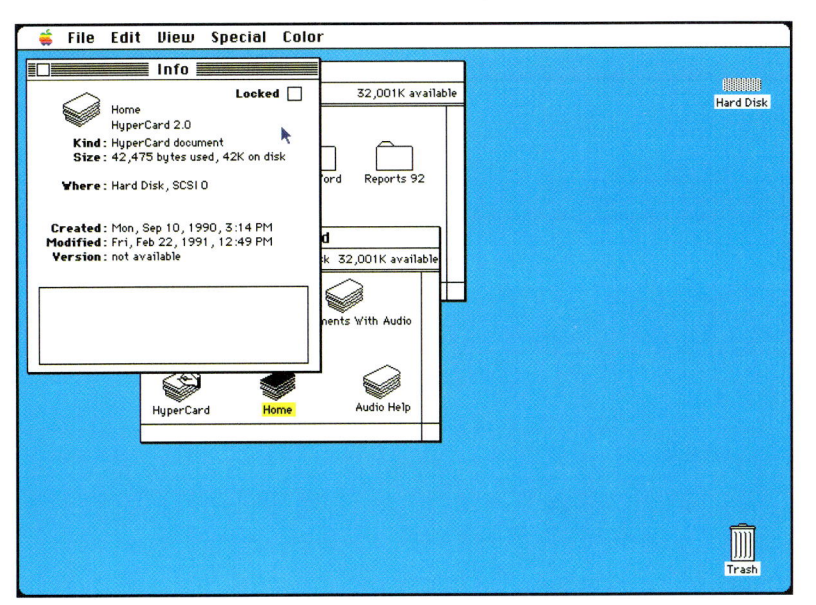

Try a shortcut
Select the document and press the ⌘-I keyboard shortcut to select the Get Info command.

after

Kind	Kind of icon; in this case, a HyperCard document
Size	The size in bytes and kilobytes (K)
Where	Location of the icon; in this case, Hard Disk
Created	Date that the document was created
Modified	Date that the document was last modified

The insertion point is located in the comment box at the bottom of the window. If you want, you can type a comment. You might, for example, make a note of what the document contains.

7. Click on the **close box**.
   This step closes the Info window.

REVIEW

1. Click on the document icon for which you want information.
2. From the **File** menu, select **Get Info**.
3. Click on the **close box**.

To display information about a document

Working with Documents and Applications

111

TASK

Lock a document

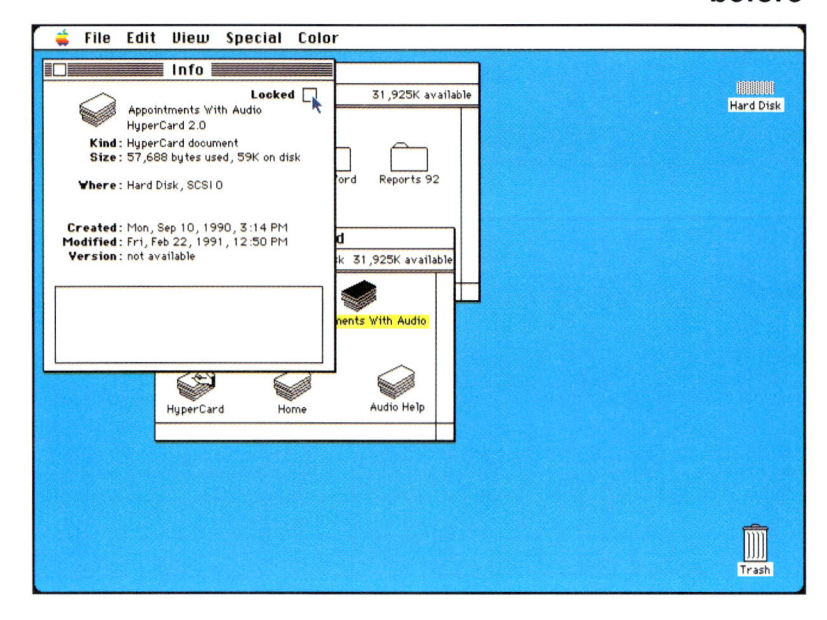

before

Oops!
Follow this same procedure to unlock the document.

1. Double-click on the **Hard Disk** icon.

   This step opens the Hard Disk window. If the window is already open, skip this step. Your hard disk might be named differently; double-click on the icon for your hard disk.

2. Double-click on the **HyperCard** icon.

   This step opens the HyperCard folder. You should have this folder. If not, open any folder.

3. Click on the **Appointments With Audio** icon.

   This step selects the Appointments With Audio document. If you don't have this document, click on one that you do have.

4. Click on **File** in the menu bar; hold down the mouse button.

   This step opens the File menu. You see a list of File commands.

5. Drag down until you highlight **Get Info**.

   This step selects the Get Info command.

6. Release the mouse button.

   You see a window that displays information about the selected item. In the upper right corner of the window, you see a check box named Locked. (The Before screen shows this step.)

112

Easy **Macintosh**

after

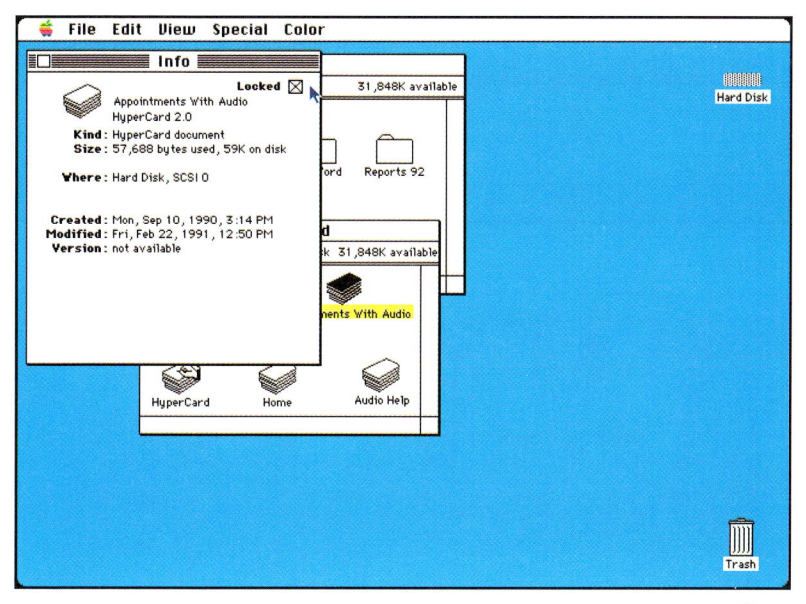

7. Click on **Locked**.
   This step locks the document. You cannot delete or change the document when the Locked check box has been checked.

8. Click on the **close box**.
   This step closes the Info window.

REVIEW

To lock a document

1. Click on the document icon that you want to lock.
2. From the **File** menu, select **Get Info**.
3. Click on the **Locked** check box.
4. Click on the **close box**.

Working with Documents and Applications

TASK

Duplicate a document

before

Oops!
As the copy is made, you see a progress window on-screen. Click on Cancel to stop the copy. If you are copying only one document, the copy might occur too quickly to cancel. In this case, delete the copy. See *TASK: Delete a document*.

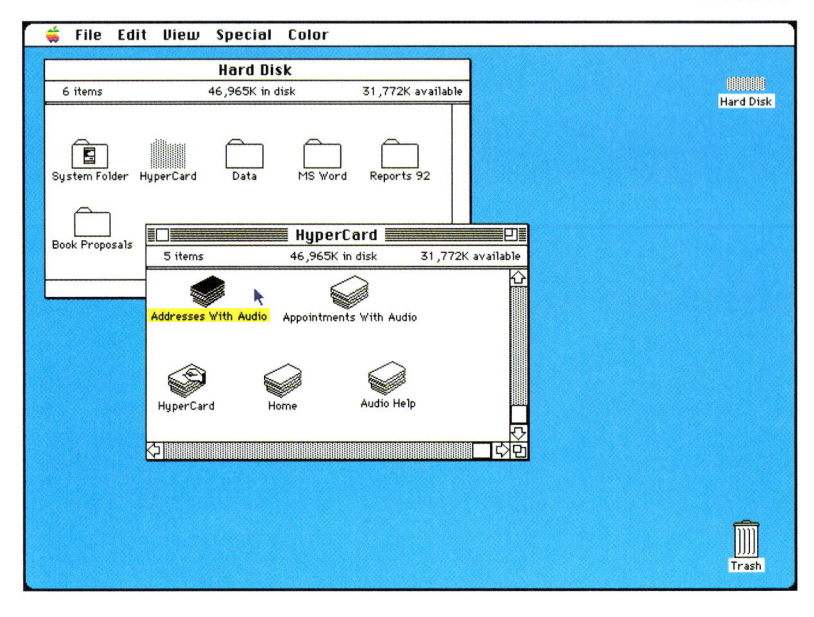

1. Double-click on the **Hard Disk** icon.

   This step opens the Hard Disk window. If the window is already open, skip this step. Your hard disk might be named differently; double-click on the icon for your hard disk.

2. Double-click on the **HyperCard** icon.

   This step opens the HyperCard folder. You should have this folder. If not, click on any folder.

3. Click on the **Addresses With Audio** icon.

   This step selects the Addresses With Audio document. If you don't have this document, select one you that do have.

4. Click on **File** in the menu bar; hold down the mouse button.

   This step opens the File menu. You see a list of File commands.

5. Drag down until you highlight **Duplicate**.

   This step selects the Duplicate command.

6. Release the mouse button.

   As the copy is made, you see a progress window on-screen. A copy is placed in the same folder and is named Copy of Addresses With Audio.

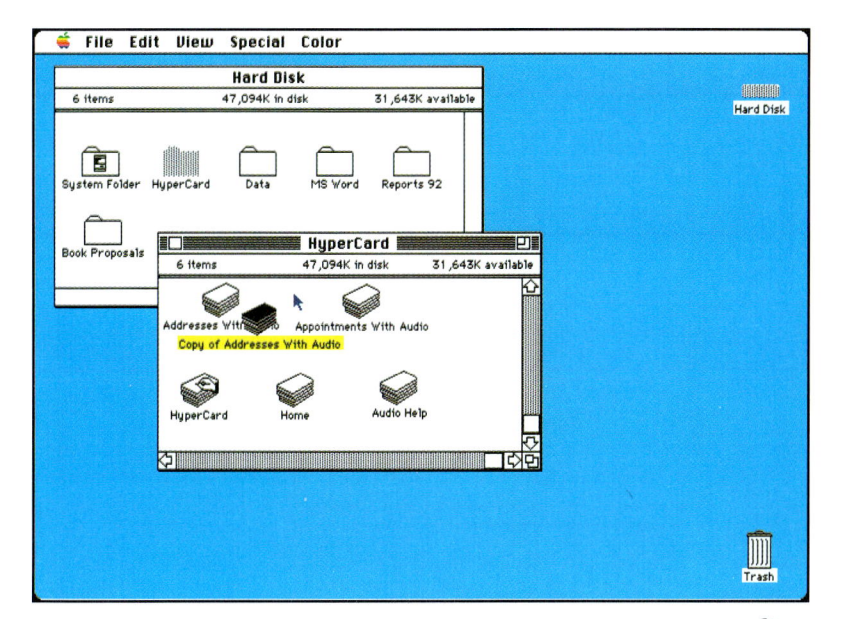

after

Try a shortcut
Press the ⌘-D keyboard combination to select the Duplicate command.

---

1. Click on the document icon that you want to copy.
2. From the **File** menu, select **Duplicate**.

REVIEW

To duplicate a document

Working with Documents and Applications

115

TASK

Rename a document

before

Oops!
To change the document back to its original name, follow this procedure.

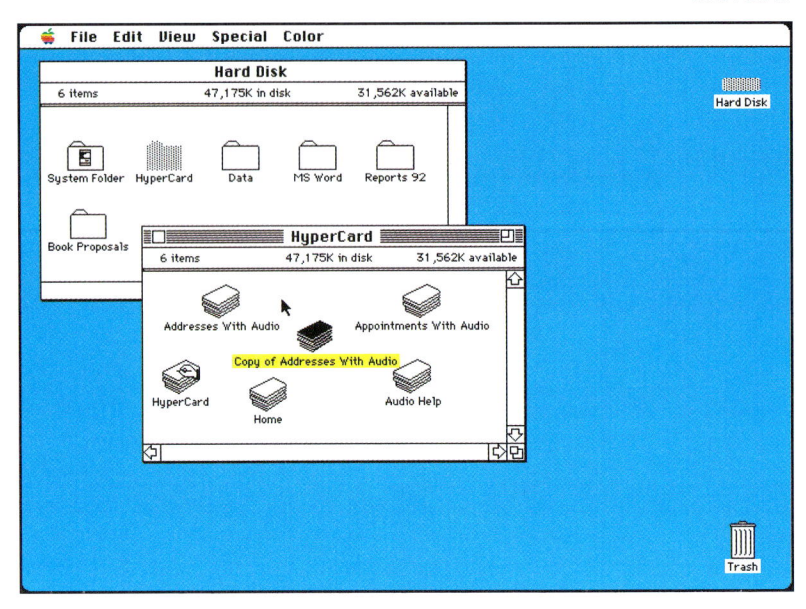

1. Double-click on the **Hard Disk** icon.

   This step opens the Hard Disk window. If the window is already open, skip this step. Your hard disk might be named differently; double-click on the icon for your hard disk.

2. Double-click on the **HyperCard** icon.

   This step opens the HyperCard folder. You should have this folder. If not, open a folder that you do have.

3. Click on the **Copy of Addresses With Audio** icon.

   This step selects the Copy of Addresses With Audio document. If you don't have this document, select one that you do have. You can move this icon so that the names don't overlap.

4. Type **Clients**.

   This is the new name for the document.

5. Press **Return**.

   This step confirms the new name.

Easy **Macintosh**

after

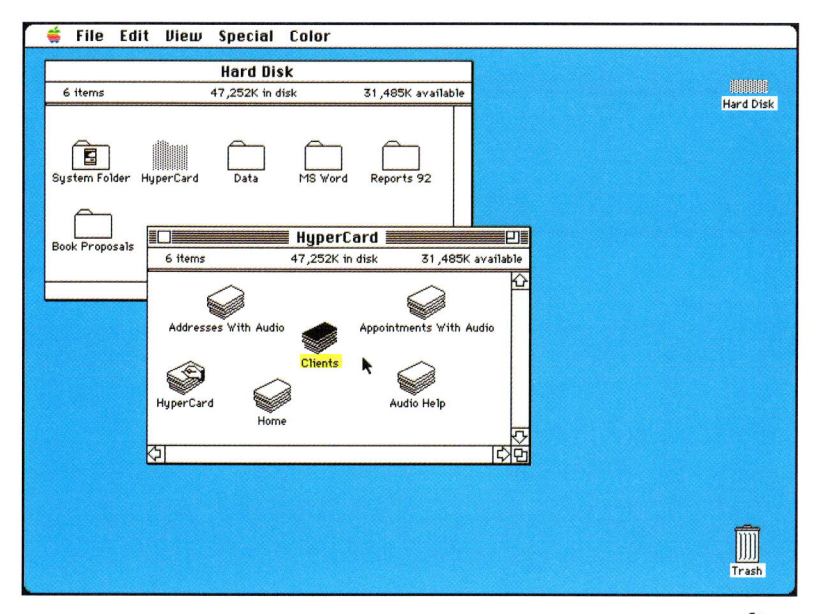

1. Click on the document icon that you want to rename.
2. Type the new name.
3. Press **Return**.

REVIEW

To rename a document

TASK

Move a document to another folder

before

Oops!
To place the document in the folder, you must be sure that the disk icon darkens. This means that the folder is selected.

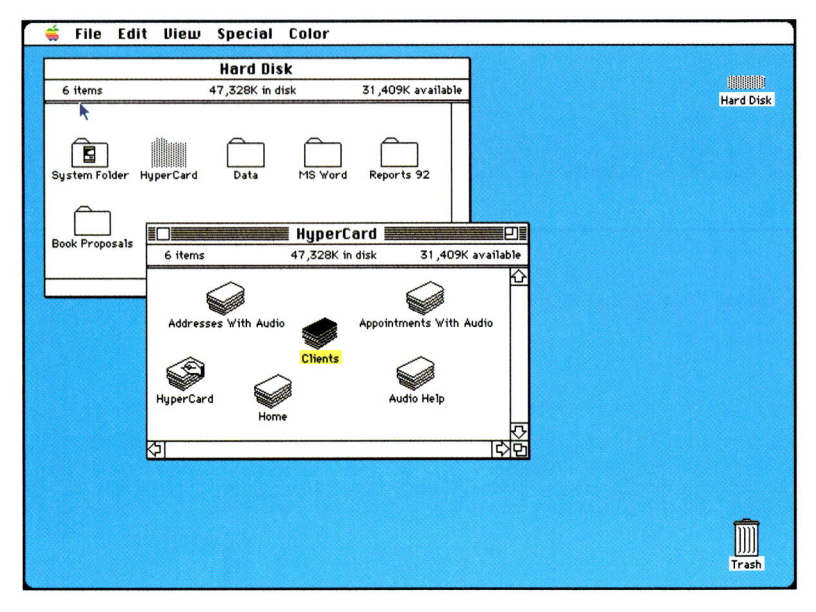

1. **Double-click on the Hard Disk icon.**

   This step opens the Hard Disk window. If the window is already open, skip this step. Your hard disk might be named differently; double-click on the icon for your hard disk.

2. **Double-click on the HyperCard icon.**

   This step opens the HyperCard folder. You should have this folder. If not, open another folder.

3. **In the HyperCard window, click on the Clients icon.**

   This step selects the Clients document. If you don't have this document, select a document that you do have. The Before screen shows this step.

4. **Hold down the mouse button and drag the document icon to the Book Proposals icon.**

   This icon appears in the hard disk window. If you don't have this folder. select one that you do have. (Do not, however, drag the document to the System Folder.) The folder icon darkens.

   You might need to move and resize the windows so that you can see both windows.

5. **Release the mouse button.**

   This step completes the move. The document no longer appears in the HyperCard window. Instead it is moved to the Book Proposals folder.

after

1. Click on the document icon you want to move; hold down the mouse button.

2. Drag the document icon onto the icon of the folder you want to move the folder to.

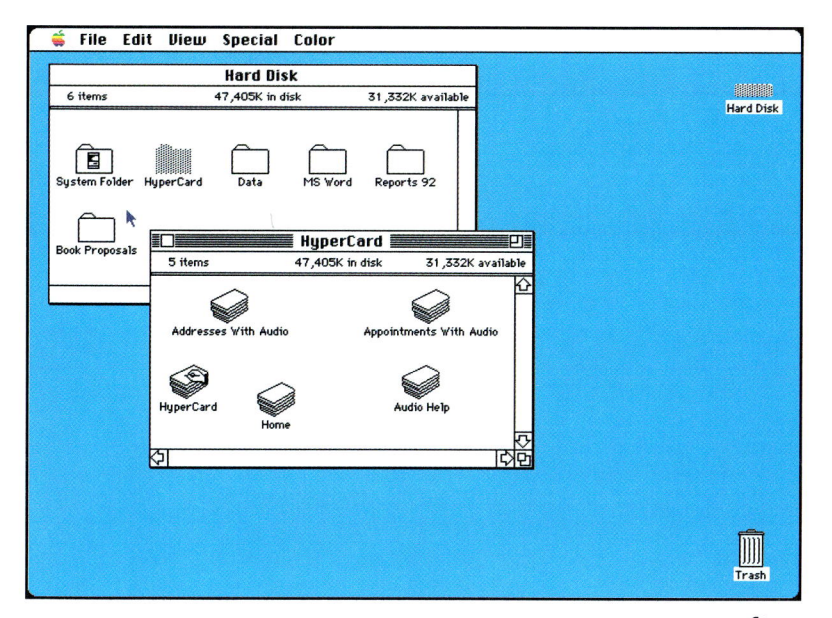

Documents have the same name?
If the document you are moving has the same name as a document in the folder to which you are moving the document, you see the message `Replace items with the same names with the selected items?` Click on OK if you want to replace the file with the updated version.

REVIEW

To move a document to another folder

Copy the document
To copy the document to another folder, see *TASK: Copy a document to another folder*.

Working with Documents and Applications

TASK

Copy a document to another folder

before

Oops!
If the document disappears from the first folder, you probably didn't press the Option key. You must press Option to tell the Macintosh that you want to copy—not move— the document.

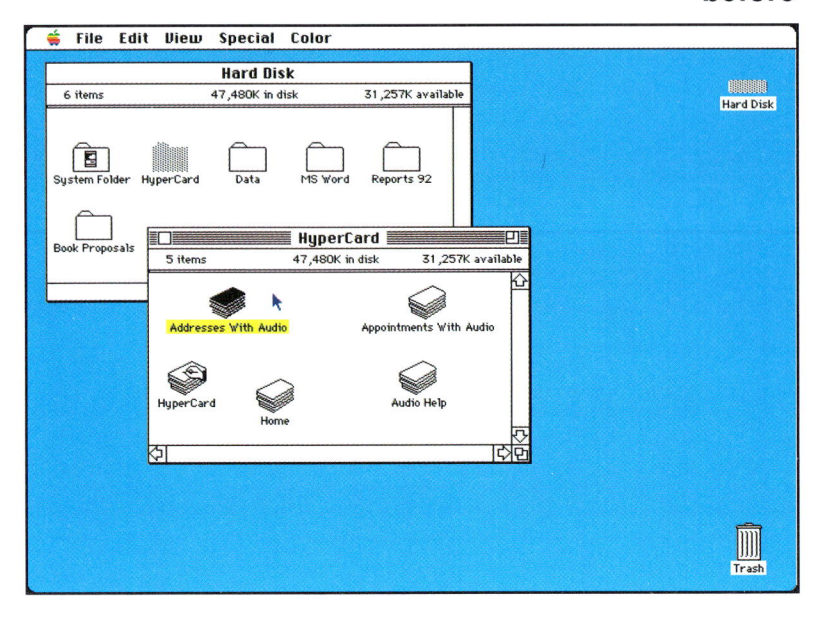

1. Double-click on the **Hard Disk** icon.

   This step opens the Hard Disk window. If the window is already open, skip this step. Your hard disk might be named differently; double-click on the icon for your hard disk.

2. Double-click on the **HyperCard** icon.

   This step opens the HyperCard folder. You should have this folder. If not, open another folder.

3. In the **HyperCard** window, click on the **Addresses With Audio** icon.

   This step selects the Addresses With Audio document. If you don't have this document, select another document. The Before screen shows this step.

4. Press and hold the **Option** key and then click and hold the mouse button.

   This step selects the file.

5. Drag the document icon to the **Book Proposals** icon.

   If you don't have this folder, select a folder that you do have. (Do not, however, drag the document to the System Folder.) The folder icon darkens.

   You might need to move and resize the windows so that you can see both windows.

Easy Macintosh

after

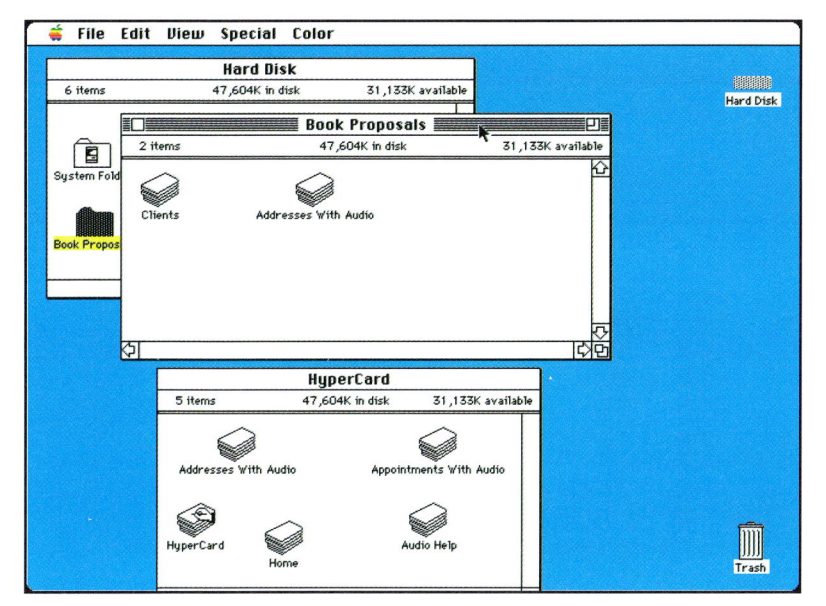

Move the document
To move the document, see *TASK: Move a document to another folder*.

6. Release the mouse button and the **Option** key.

   This step completes the copy. The document appears in the HyperCard window and the Book Proposals folder.

7. Double-click on the **Book Proposals** icon.

   This step opens the folder window so that you can verify a copy was made. You might need to move and resize the windows so that you can see both windows. This copy has the same name as the original.

REVIEW

To copy a document to another folder

1. Click on the document icon you want to copy.

2. Hold down the mouse button and press and hold the **Option** key.

3. Drag the document icon onto the folder icon.

4. Release the mouse button and the **Option** key.

Working with Documents and Applications

121

TASK

Copy a document to another disk

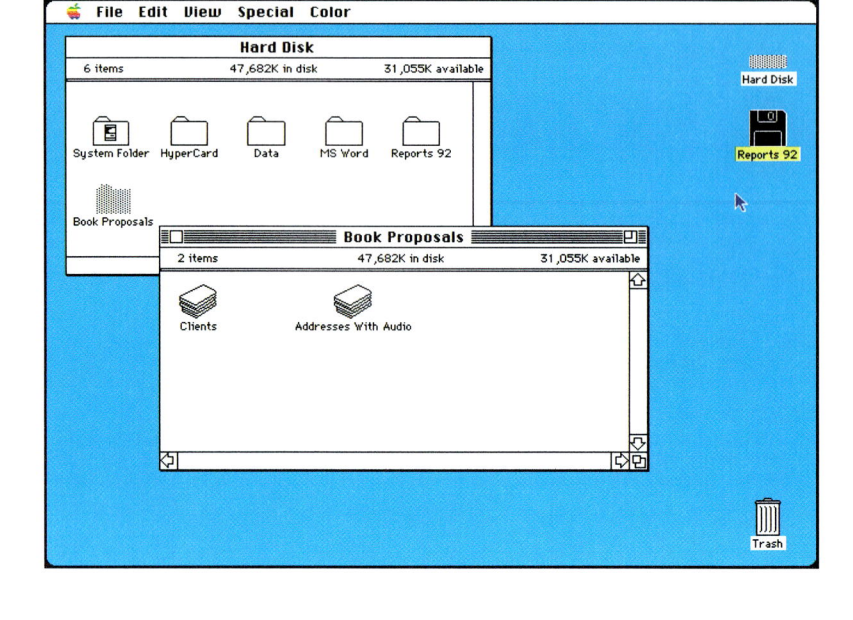

before

Oops!
If the document icon is only moved (not copied), you did not place it on the disk. Be sure that the disk darkens when the document icon is placed on the disk.

1. Double-click on the **Hard Disk** icon.

    This step opens the Hard Disk window. If the window is already open, skip this step. Your hard disk might be named differently; double-click on the icon for your hard disk.

2. Double-click on the **Book Proposals** icon.

    This step opens the Book Proposals folder. If you don't have this folder, select a folder that you do have. (Do not, however, select the System Folder.)

3. Insert the **Reports 92** disk.

    If you don't have this disk, insert another disk.

4. In the **Book Proposals** window, click on the **Addresses With Audio** icon.

    This step selects the Addresses With Audio document. (If you don't have this document, select a document that you do have.)

5. Hold down the mouse button and drag the document icon to the **Reports 92** icon.

    The disk icon darkens.

Easy **Macintosh**

after

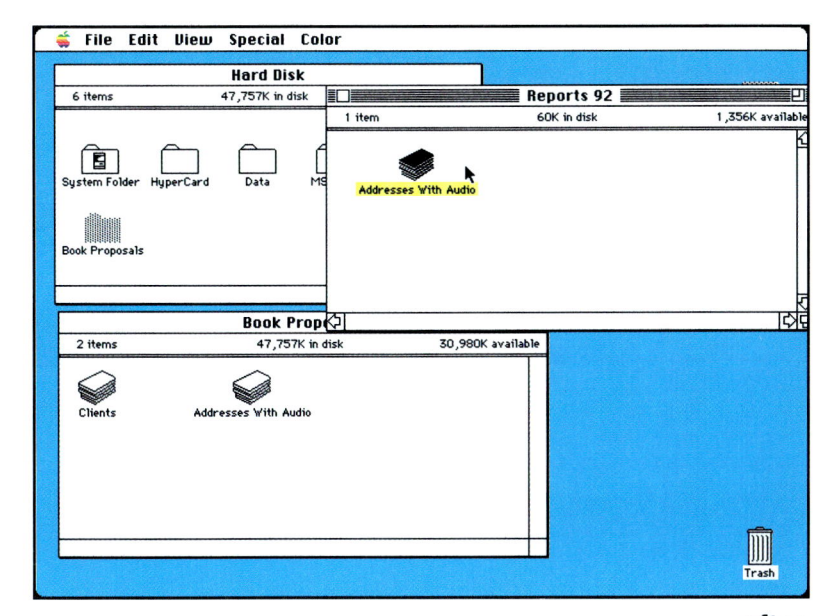

Delete the document
To delete the copy, see
TASK: *Delete a document*.

6. Release the mouse button.

   This step completes the copy. To see the copy, open the disk icon.

7. Double-click on the **Reports 92** icon.

   This step opens the Reports 92 disk window so that you can verify that the document was copied. The document appears in both locations: in the Book Proposals folder and on the Reports 92 disk. You might need to move and resize the windows so that you can see both windows.

REVIEW

1. Click on the document icon you want to copy; hold down the mouse button.

2. Drag the document icon onto the disk icon.

To copy a document to another disk

Working with Documents and Applications

123

TASK

Delete a document

before

Oops!
If the Trash has not been emptied (see *TASK: Empty the Trash*), you can retrieve the document. See *TASK: Retrieve an item from the Trash can icon*.

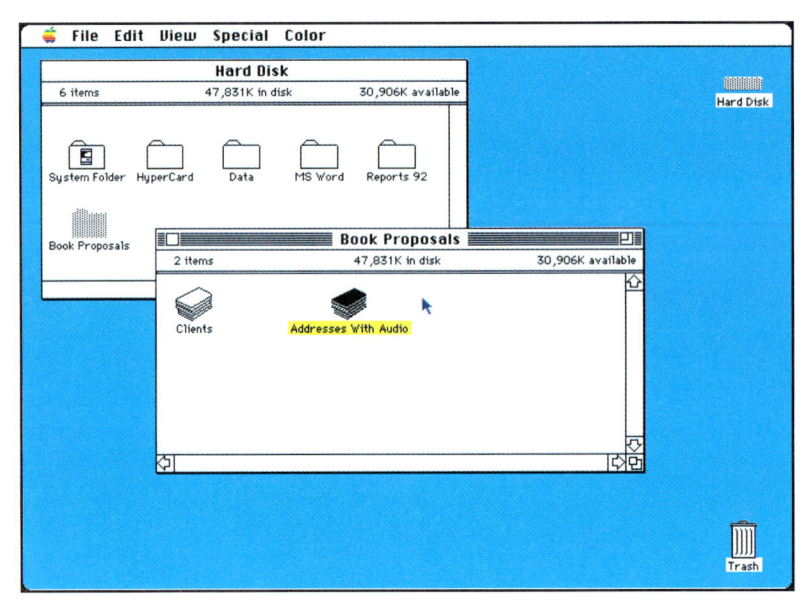

1. Double-click on the **Hard Disk** icon.

   This step opens the Hard Disk window. If the window is already open, skip this step. Your hard disk might be named differently; double-click on the icon for your hard disk.

2. Double-click on the **Book Proposals** icon.

   This steps opens the folder window. You see the documents that this folder contains.

3. Point to **Addresses With Audio** icon.

   If you don't have this document, click on a document that you do have. Be sure to select one that you don't need.

4. Click and hold down the mouse button, and then drag the document to the **Trash can** icon.

   This step places the document in the Trash. The Trash can icon darkens.

5. Release the mouse button.

   This step completes the deletion. (You can tell that the item is in the Trash because the sides of the Trash can icon bulge.)

124

Easy **Macintosh**

after

1. Point to the document icon that you want to delete.
2. Click and hold down the mouse button.
3. Drag the document icon to the **Trash can** icon.
4. Release the mouse button.

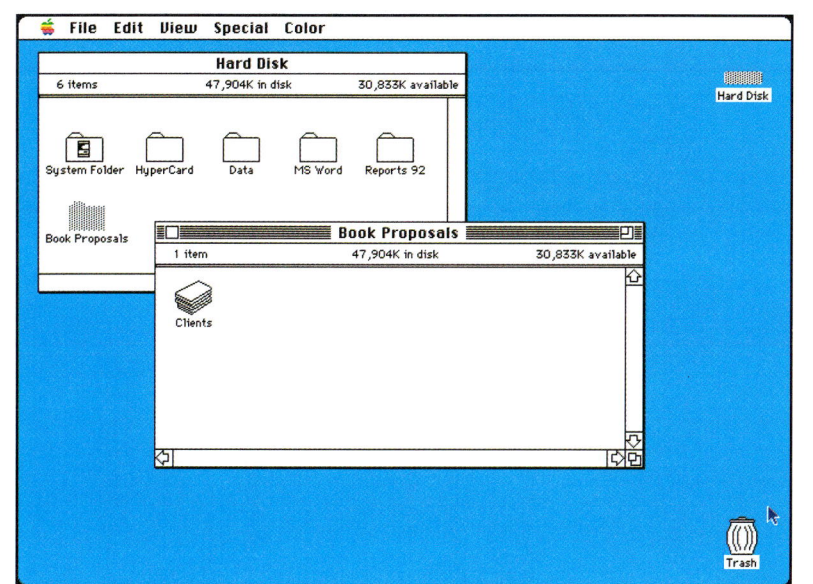

Be careful!
Don't delete a document that you need. If the Trash has been emptied, the document will be lost.

REVIEW

To delete a document

TASK

Find a document

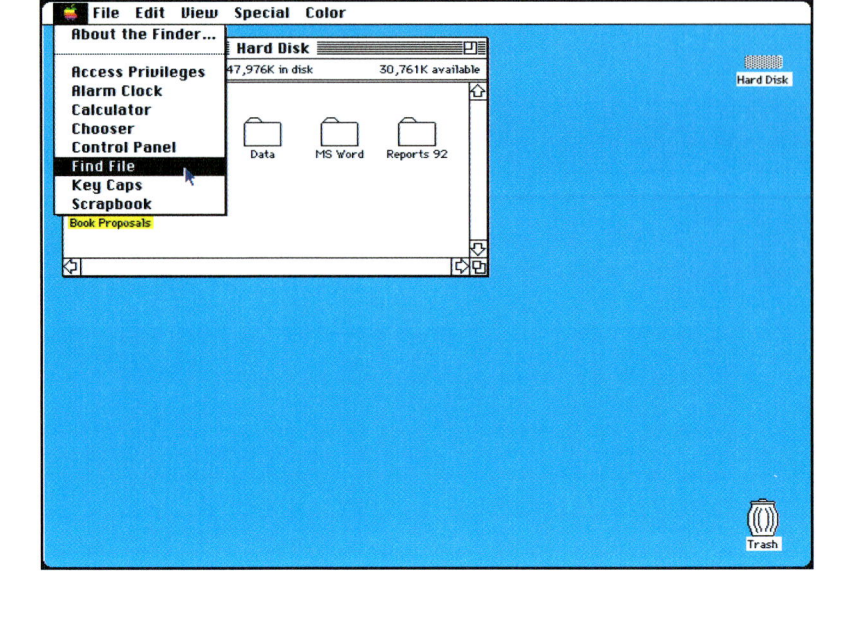

before

Oops!
If no matching items are found, you hear the alert sound. Try the search again.

1. Click on in the menu bar; hold down the mouse button.

   This command opens the menu. You see a list of commands.

2. Drag down until you highlight **Find File**.

   This command selects the Find File accessory. To search for files, you use a special desk accessory.

   You see the Find File window. The first item lists the name of the hard disk—the item to be searched. (You can click on this item to change the item that is searched.)

   The insertion point blinks in the Search for box; this is where you type the file name you want to find.

3. Type **Home**.

   This is the item for which you want to search.

4. Click on the **running man** icon.

   This step starts the search. The files that are found—Home, in this case—appear in the middle box. You hear the alert sound.

5. Click on the name of the file that has been found (**Home**).

   This step displays information about the found file. In the lower left box, you see information about when the file was created,

Easy **Macintosh**

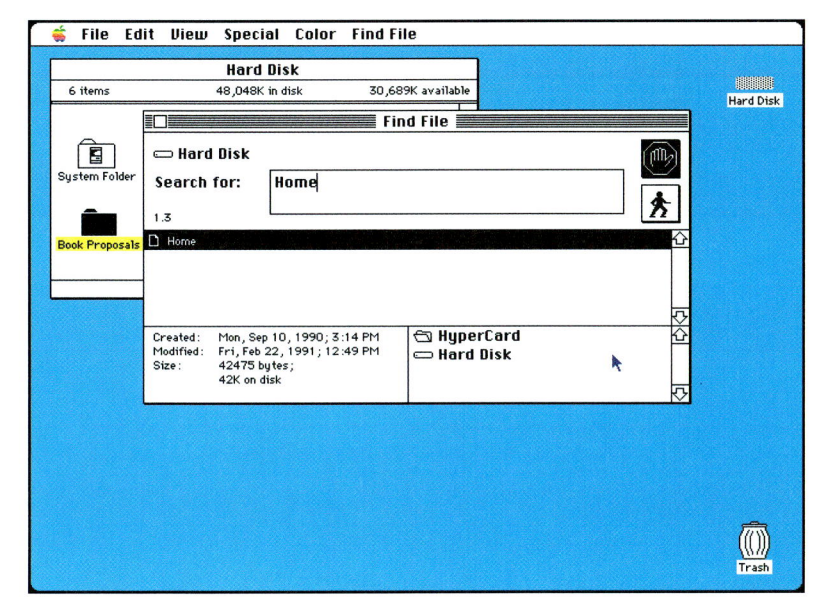

after

Open the file
Keep in mind that Find File does just that—finds the file. It does not open the file. To open the file, return to the Desktop and open the file.

when the file was modified, and the size of the file. In the lower right box you see the location of the file. The folder that contains the file is listed first, followed by the hard disk (which contains the folder).

6. Click on the **close box**.
   This step closes the File Find window.

REVIEW

1. From the menu, select **Find File**.
2. Type the name of the document in the Find File window.
3. Click on the **running man** icon.

To find a document

Working with Documents and Applications

Working with Accessories

This section covers the following tasks:

Change the Desktop pattern

Change the speaker volume

Change the date

Change the time

Change the alert sound

Display the time

Set an alarm

Use the Calculator

Display a special character

TASK

Change the Desktop pattern

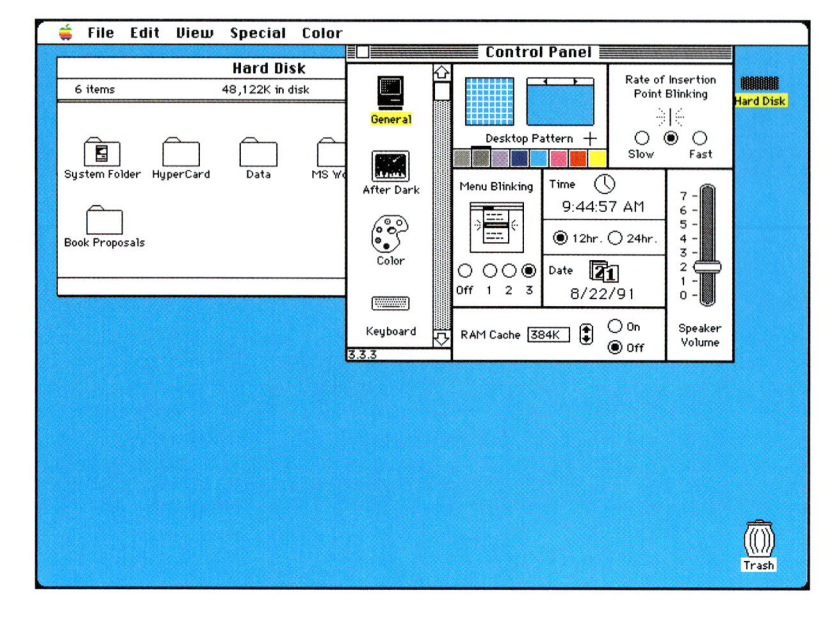

before

Oops!
If you return to the Desktop and don't see any change, you probably forgot to click on the middle of the Desktop (step 5 of the Task section) to apply the change. Try this procedure again.

1. Click on in the menu bar; hold down the mouse button.

   This step opens the menu. You see a list of desk accessories (DAs). A desk accessory is a small program—usually created to perform a single function (such as display the time). Some desk accessories come with the Macintosh. You can purchase other desk accessories.

2. Drag down until you highlight **Control Panel**.

   This step selects the Control Panel accessory. Use this accessory to change settings for the Macintosh.

3. Release the mouse button.

   You see a window with control panel settings. General is selected in the left side of the window. Options include changing the Desktop pattern, changing the speaker volume, and setting menu blinking.

   Note that the Desktop Pattern box is in the upper middle portion of the window. You see two items inside this area. The first item is a small square that represents a small square of the Desktop. The second item represents the entire Desktop. Above this item you see two arrows.

130

Easy **Macintosh**

after

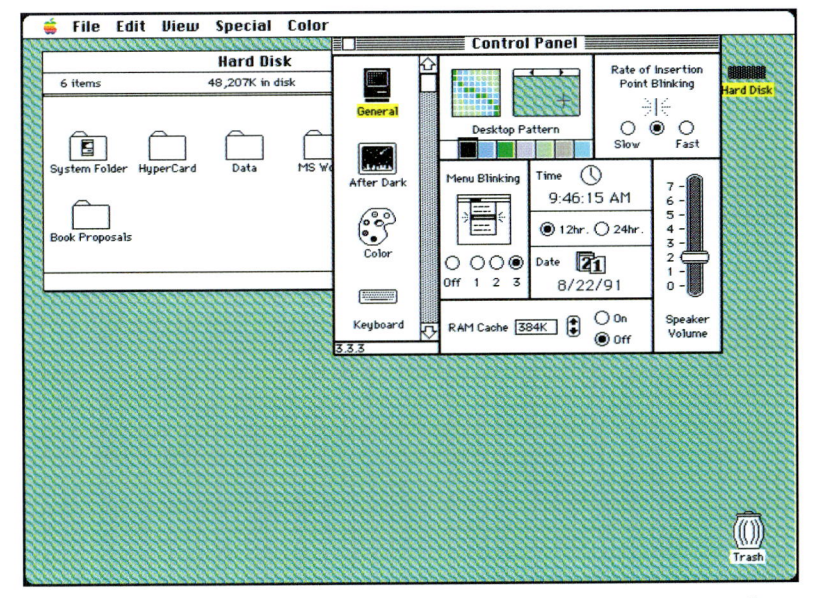

4. Click on ▶ until you see a pattern you like.

   As you click on ▶, the pattern changes—both in the small square and the Desktop. Around 10-15 preselected color patterns are provided with the color Macintoshes.

5. Click on the representation of the Desktop.

   Click on the Desktop in the window on-screen—not the actual Desktop. This step applies the change.

6. Click on the **close box**.

   This step closes the Control Panel window.

Edit the pattern
You also can create your own pattern by clicking in the small sample area. Clicking on a spot turns the spot to the selected color; clicking on it again makes the spot white.

Return to the original pattern
To return to the original pattern, follow this procedure. If you created the pattern from scratch, you will have to create the original pattern again.

REVIEW

1. From the menu, select **Control Panel**.
2. Click on ▶ or ◀, above the small Desktop, until the pattern you want appears.
3. Click on the representation of the Desktop.
4. Click on the **close box**.

To change the Desktop pattern

Working with Accessories

131

TASK

Change the speaker volume

before

Oops!
If you don't hear alert sounds, the volume might be set to 0. Follow these steps to check the volume.

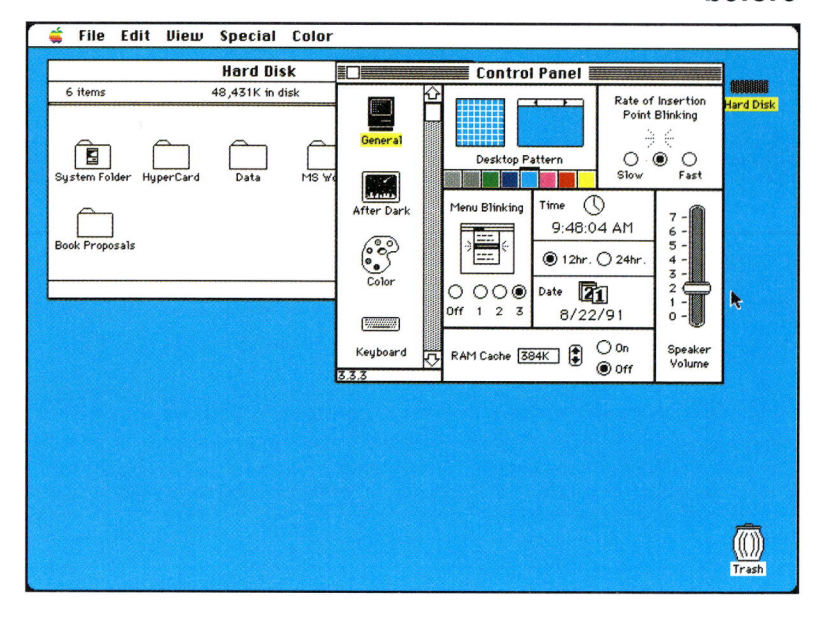

1. Click on in the menu bar; hold down the mouse button.

   This step opens the menu. You see a list of desk accessories.

2. Drag down until you highlight **Control Panel**.

   This step selects the Control Panel accessory. Use this accessory to change settings for the Macintosh.

3. Release the mouse button.

   You see a window with control panel settings. General is selected in the left side of the window. Options include changing the Desktop pattern, changing the speaker volume, and setting menu blinking.

   Note that the Speaker volume box is in the lower right side of the window. The volume levels go from 0 (no sound) to 7. A volume bar indicates the current volume level.

4. Click on the **volume bar** and hold down the mouse button.

   This step selects the volume bar.

5. Drag the volume bar until the volume is set to 7.

   This is the new volume.

after

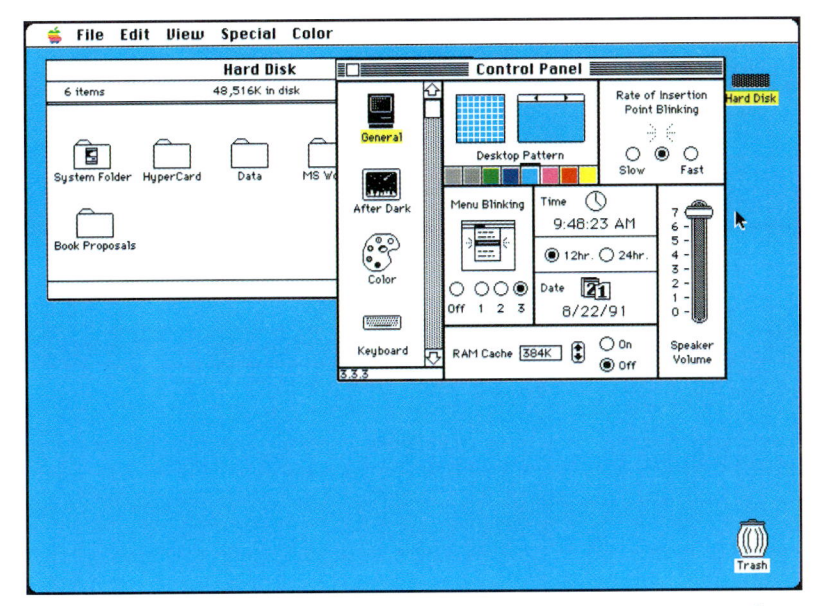

Change the alert sound
You can change the alert sound. See *TASK: Change the alert sound.*

6. Release the mouse button.

   You hear the alert sound—a beep—at the new volume. (You might hear a different alert sound.)

7. Click on the **close box**.

   This step closes the Control Panel window.

REVIEW

To change the speaker volume

1. From the menu, select **Control Panel**.

2. Click on the **volume bar** in the Speaker Volume part of the window; hold down the mouse button.

3. Drag the volume bar to a new level.

4. Release the mouse button.

5. Click on the **close box**.

Working with Accessories

TASK

Change the date

before

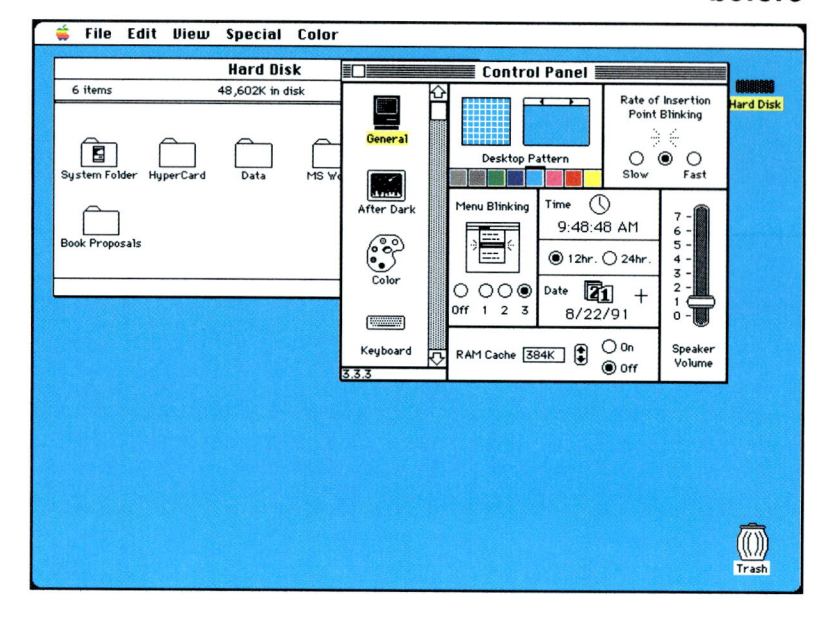

Oops!
Follow this same procedure to change the date back to the original setting.

1. Click on in the menu bar; hold down the mouse button.

   This step opens the menu. You see a list of desk accessories.

2. Drag down until you highlight **Control Panel**.

   This step selects the Control Panel accessory. Use this accessory to change settings for the Macintosh.

3. Release the mouse button.

   You see a window with control panel settings. General is selected in the left side of the window. Options include changing the Desktop pattern, changing the speaker volume, and setting menu blinking.

   A box for the date is located in the middle of the window.

4. Click on the year.

   This step selects the year. The year appears in reverse video. (In the Before figure, the year is 91.) You also can click on the month or the day to change these settings. The pointer becomes a cross bar, and arrows appear to the right of the date.

5. Click on .

   This step adds a year to the date.

6. Click on the **close box**.

   This step closes the Control Panel window.

Easy **Macintosh**

after

REVIEW

To change the date

1. From the menu, select **Control Panel**.

2. Click on the part of the date you want to change—month, day, or year.

3. Click on ↑ to increase the date; click on ↓ to decrease the date.

4. Click on the **close box**.

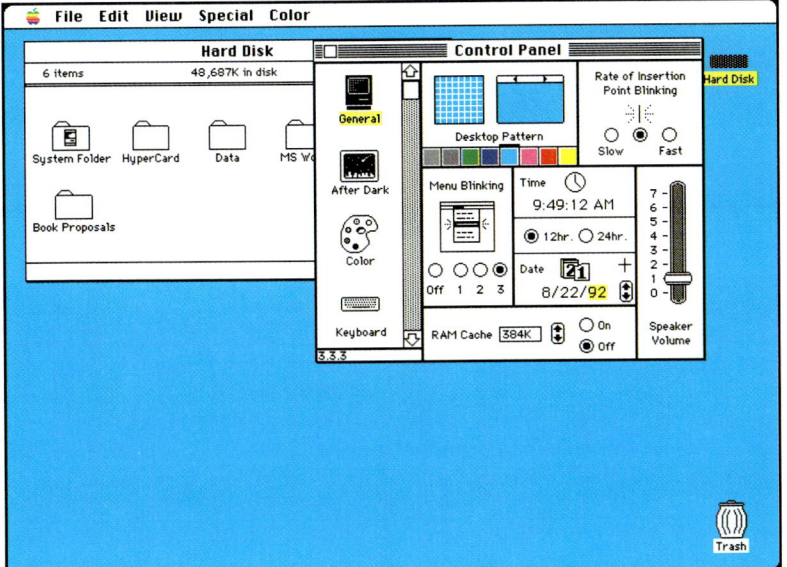

Be careful!
The Macintosh uses this date to keep track of when documents are modified. Be sure to enter the correct date.

Try a shortcut
When you highlight the part you want to change, just type the text for that area, and then press the key to move to the next area.

Working with Accessories

135

TASK

Change the time

before

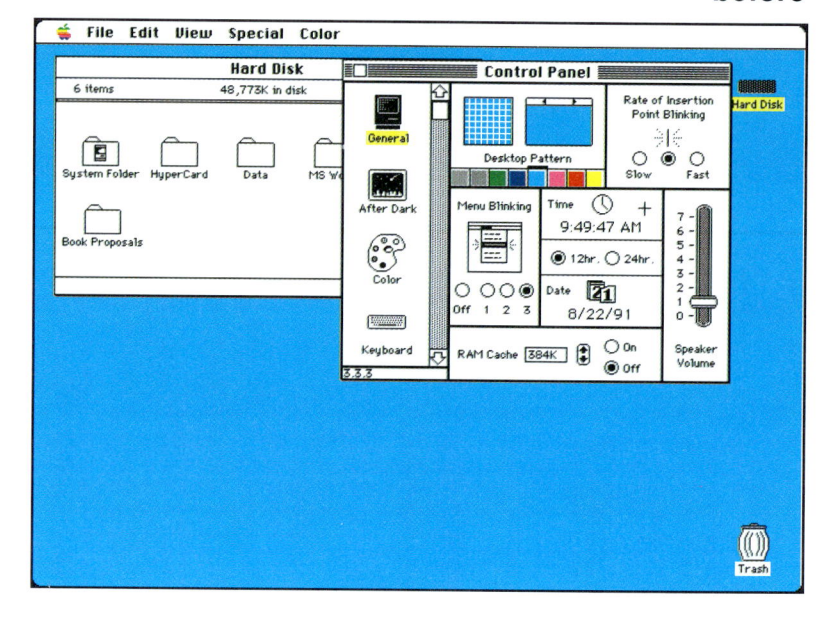

Oops!
Follow this same procedure to change the time back to the original setting.

1. Click on in the menu bar; hold down the mouse button.

   This step opens the menu. You see a list of desk accessories.

2. Drag down until you highlight **Control Panel**.

   This step selects the Control Panel accessory. Use this accessory to change settings for the Macintosh.

3. Release the mouse button.

   You see a window with control panel settings. General is selected in the left side of the window. Options include changing the Desktop pattern, changing the speaker volume, and setting menu blinking.

   A box for the time is located in the middle of the screen.

4. Click on the hour.

   This step selects the hour. The hour appears in reverse video. (In the Before figure, the hour is 9.) You can also click on the minutes or seconds to change these settings. Arrows appear to the right of the time.

5. Click on ⬇.

   This step decreases the hour by one (the time is earlier).

6. Click on the **close box**.

   This step closes the Control Panel.

Easy **Macintosh**

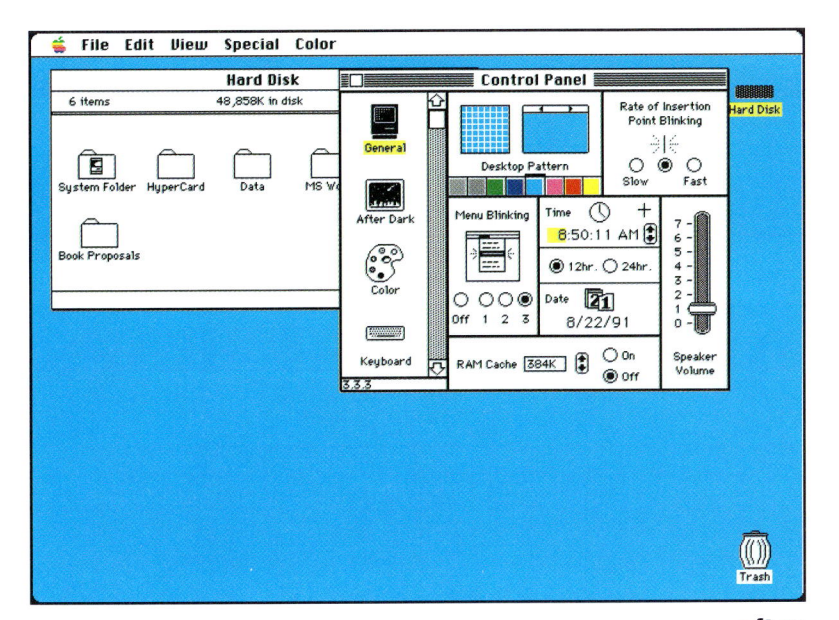

after

1. From the menu, select **Control Panel**.

2. Click on the part of the time you want to change—hour, minutes, or seconds.

3. Click on ↑ to increase the time; click on ↓ to decrease the time.

4. Click on the **close box**.

Be careful!
The Macintosh uses the time to keep track of when documents are created and modified. Be sure to enter the correct time.

REVIEW

To change the time

Change the time format
In the Control Panel window, you also can select 12 hr for a 12-hour clock or 24 hr for a 24-hour clock (military time). Click on the button located below the time setting.

Working with Accessories

137

TASK

Change the alert sound

before

Oops!
If you don't hear alert sounds, the volume might be set to 0. Check the volume.

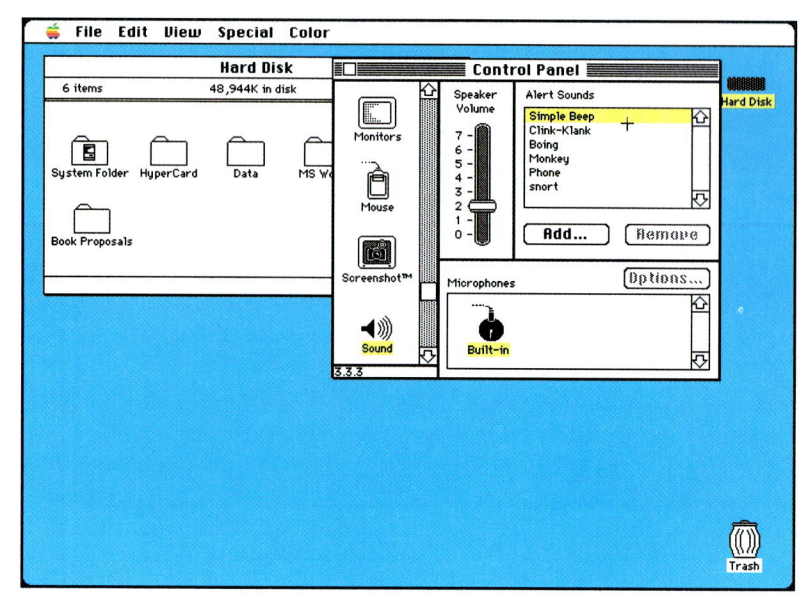

1. **Click on in the menu bar; hold down the mouse button.**

   This step opens the menu. You see a list of desk accessories.

2. **Drag down until you highlight Control Panel.**

   This step selects the Control Panel accessory. Use this accessory to change settings for the Macintosh.

3. **Release the mouse button.**

   You see a window with control panel settings. The left side of the window displays the different control panels.

4. **Click on Sound.**

   This step selects the Sound control panel. (You might have to click on the scroll arrows in the middle of the screen to display this option.)

   On the right side of the window, you see a list of alert sounds.

5. **Click on Boing.**

   This step selects the sound. You hear *Boing*. Depending on your Macintosh, you may have different sounds. If you don't have Boing, choose another sound from the list.

6. **Click on the close box.**

   This step closes the control panel window.

138

Easy **Macintosh**

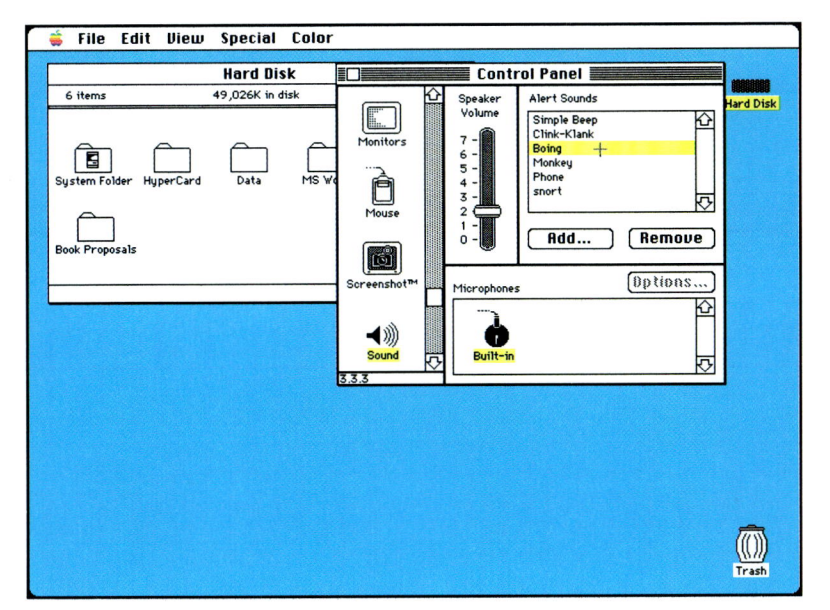

Change the volume
You also can change the volume with the Sound control panel. Click on the speaker bar, hold down the mouse button, and drag to a new volume.

after

REVIEW

1. From the menu, select **Control Panel**.
2. Click on **Sound**.
3. Click on the sound you want.
4. Click on the **close box**.

To change the alert sound

Working with Accessories

139

TASK

Display the time

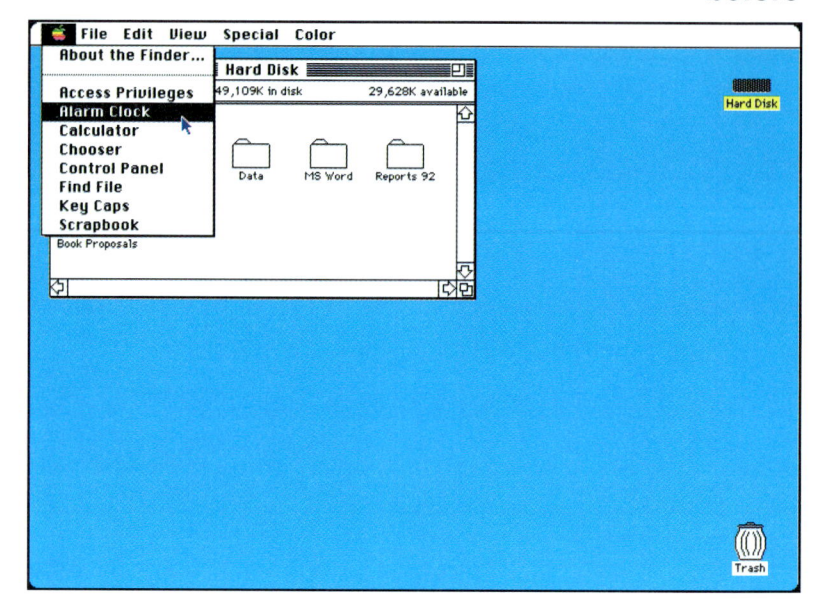

before

Oops!
Click on the close box to close the Alarm Clock window.

1. Click on in the menu bar; hold down the mouse button.

   This step opens the menu. You see a list of desk accessories.

2. Drag down until you highlight **Alarm Clock**.

   This step selects the Alarm Clock desk accessory.

3. Release the mouse button.

   You see a window that displays the current time.

4. Click on the lever to the right of the time.

   This step expands the box to show the date. (You can change the date and time and set the alarm in this expanded box.)

after

From the menu, select **Alarm Clock**.

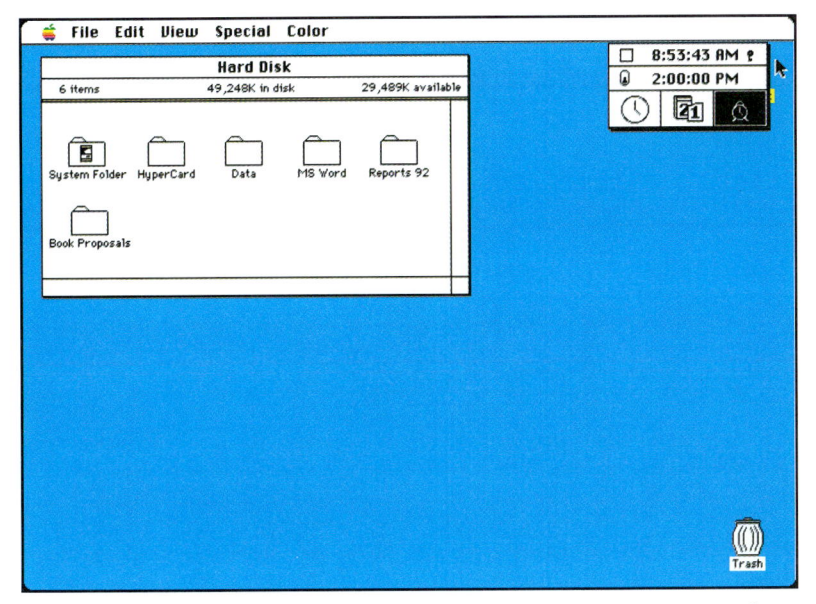

REVIEW

To display the time

Working with Accessories

141

TASK

Set an alarm

before

Oops!
To turn off the alarm, display the expanded alarm box, click on the alarm switch (in the down position), and click on the close box to close the alarm clock.

1. Click on in the menu bar; hold down the mouse button.

   This step opens the menu. You see a list of desk accessories.

2. Drag down until you highlight **Alarm Clock**.

   This step selects the Alarm Clock accessory.

3. Release the mouse button.

   You see a window displaying the current time.

4. Click on the lever to the right of the time.

   This step expands the box to show the date and time. The Before screen shows this step.

5. Click on the **alarm clock**.

   The alarm clock is in the right corner of the expanded box.

6. Click on the hour.

   This hour control is the middle of the expanded box. (In the Before figure, the hour is 9.)

after

7. Click on ↑ until the hour reads 12.

    This step sets the alarm at 12:00:00.

8. Click on the **alarm switch**.

    The alarm switch is located in the middle part of the box. It should be in the up position, and the alarm clock shows a ringing alarm, which tells you that the alarm is set.

    At the set time, the alarm will sound—you hear the alert sound, and an alarm clock flashes over the menu.

REVIEW

To set an alarm

1. From the menu, select **Alarm Clock**.
2. Click on the lever to the right of the time.
3. Click on the **alarm clock**.
4. Set the time you want the alarm to sound.
5. Click on the **alarm switch**.

Working with Accessories

TASK

Use the calculator

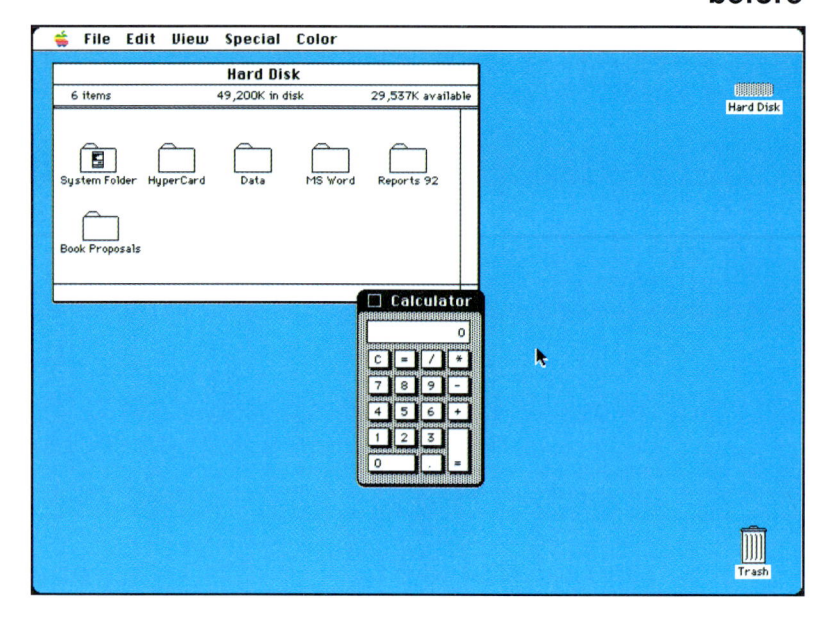

before

Oops!
If you press the Return key, you hear the alert sound. You must press = (equal) or Enter.

1. Click on in the menu bar; hold down the mouse button.

   This step opens the menu. You see a list of desk accessories.

2. Drag down until you highlight **Calculator**.

   This step selects the Calculator desk accessory.

3. Release the mouse button.

   You see an on-screen version of a calculator.

4. Type **50**.

   Use the numbers on the numeric keypad. 50 is the first value of the calculation. (You enter calculations just like you do with a hand-held calculator. This example shows a simple multiplication formula.)

5. Press *****.

   This step tells the Calculator to perform a multiplication formula.

6. Type **.15**.

   This step completes the formula (50 multiplied by .15).

7. Press **Enter** on the numeric keypad.

   You see the results on the entry line—in this case, 7.5. You also can press the equal sign to see the results.

144

Easy **Macintosh**

after

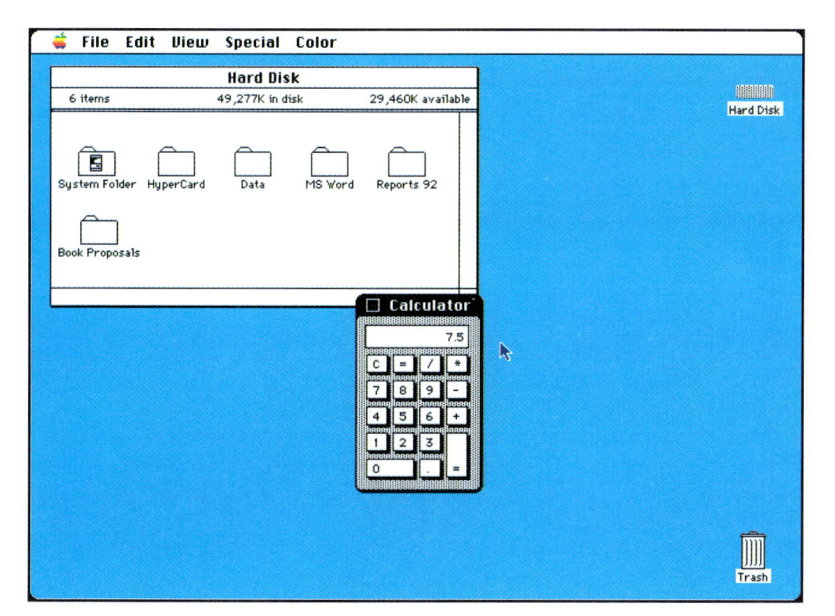

Close the calculator
Click on the close box to close the calculator.

REVIEW

1. From the menu, select **Calculator**.
2. Type the equation.
3. Press **Enter** on the numeric keypad.

To use the calculator

Use the mouse
You also can use the mouse to enter numbers. Just click on the on-screen calculation buttons.

Working with Accessories

145

TASK

Display a special character

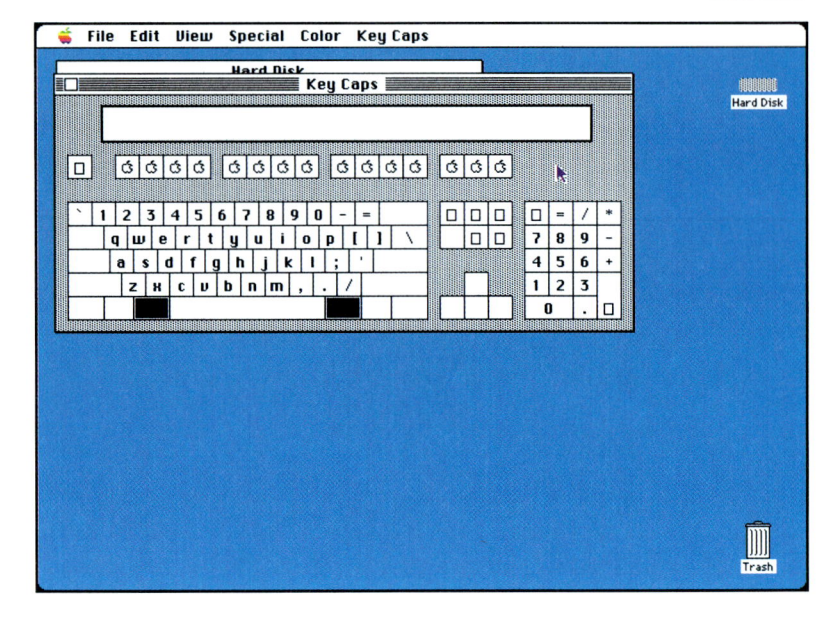

before

Oops!
Be sure to hold down the first key while pressing the second key.

1. Click on in the menu bar; hold down the mouse button.

   This step opens the menu. You see a list of desk accessories.

2. Drag down until you highlight **Key Caps**.

   This step selects the Key Caps desk accessory.

3. Release the mouse button.

   You see an on-screen version of the keyboard. The top part of the window includes a box for you to type characters.

4. Press and hold the **Ctrl** key.

   The keyboard changes to display other characters. The keyboard will display different characters, depending on the font you have selected and the key you press.

5. Type **T**.

   You see the symbol in the entry window.

after

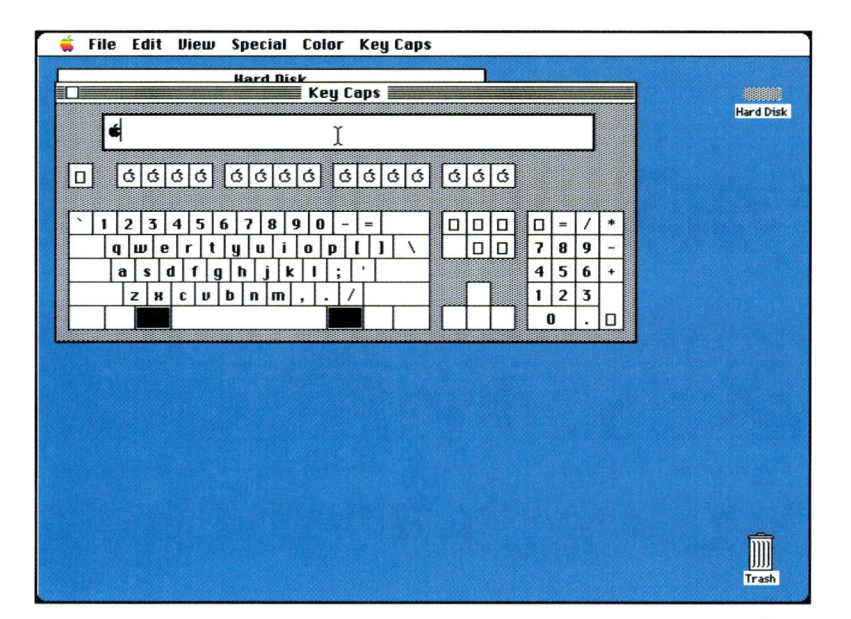

Close Key Caps
To close the Key Caps desk accessory, click on the close box.

REVIEW

1. From the menu, select **Key Caps**.

2. Press and hold the **Ctrl**, **Option**, or **Shift key** to see what characters are available.

3. If you want to display the character in the entry box, press the letter of the character you want.

To display a special character

Working with Accessories

147

Working with HyperCard Stacks

This section covers the following tasks:
Open the Addresses With Audio stack
Quit HyperCard
Add a new address card
Display a different address card
Find an address card
Add a note to an address card
Edit an address card
Delete an address card
Open the Appointments With Audio stack
Display a different appointment date
Add an appointment
Find an appointment card
Add a note to an appointment card
Edit an appointment card
Delete an appointment

TASK

Open the Addresses With Audio stack

before

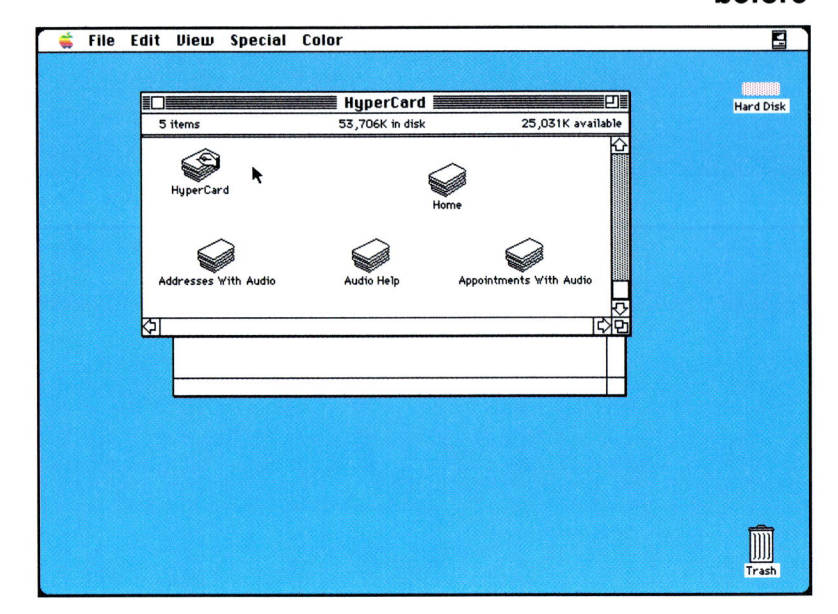

Oops!
To close the HyperCard stack, see *TASK: Quit HyperCard*.

1. **Open the HyperCard folder.**

   For help with this step, see *TASK: Open a folder*. You see a window with several different stacks. A HyperCard stack is a collection of cards.

2. **Double-click on the Addresses With Audio icon.**

   This step opens the Addresses With Audio stack. This HyperCard stack is supplied with the Macintosh. If you do not have this stack, skip this and all the other address tasks in this section.

   You see an on-screen version of an address book. A sample entry appears with entries for the name, company, address, and telephone number.

   Buttons appear to the right of the address card. These buttons let you find a card, add notes, delete a card, and move among cards. (See the other tasks in this section.)

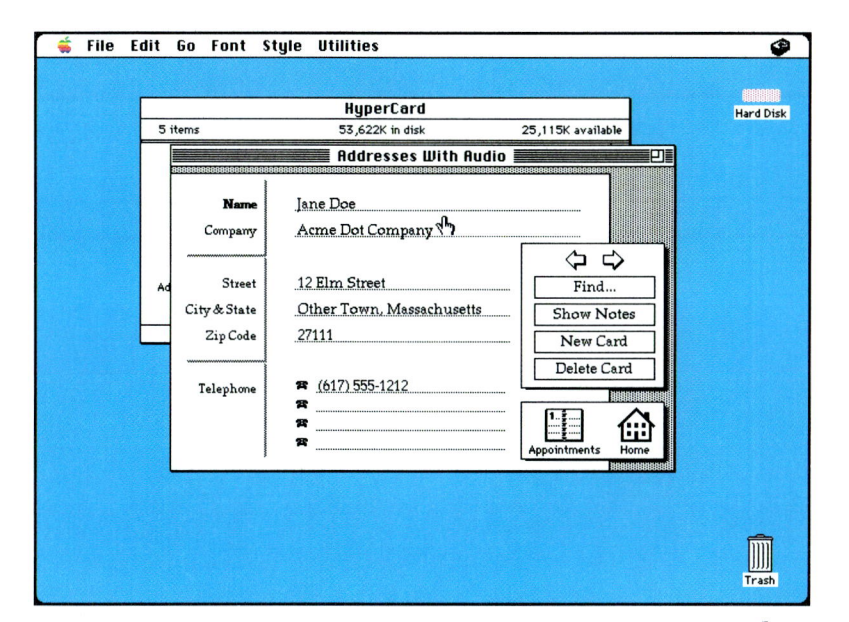

after

1. Open the **HyperCard folder**.
2. Double-click on the **Addresses With Audio** icon.

Don't have HyperCard or the stacks?
If you don't have HyperCard or the stacks mentioned here, you cannot complete this or any of the other tasks in this section.

REVIEW

To open the Addresses With Audio stack

What is HyperCard?
HyperCard is a complete application with its own menu system. For help with all HyperCard tasks, see Que's *HyperCard 2 QuickStart*.

Working with HyperCard Stacks

151

TASK

Quit HyperCard

before

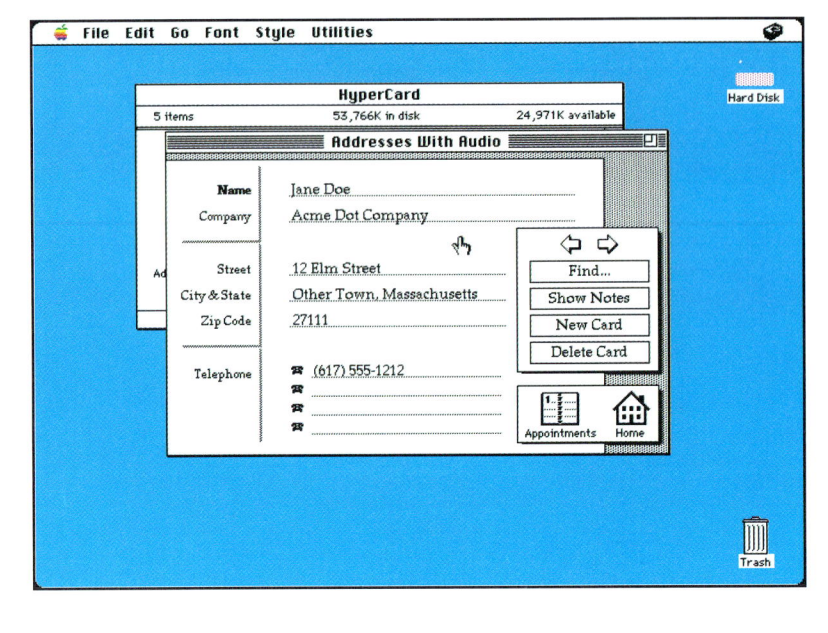

Oops!
To reopen a stack, see *TASK: Open the Addresses With Audio stack* or *TASK: Open the Appointments With Audio stack*.

1. Click on **File** in the menu bar; hold down the mouse button.
   This step opens the File menu. You see a list of File commands.

2. Drag down until you highlight **Quit HyperCard**.
   This step selects the Quit HyperCard command.

3. Release the mouse button.
   This step closes the HyperCard stack and quits HyperCard.

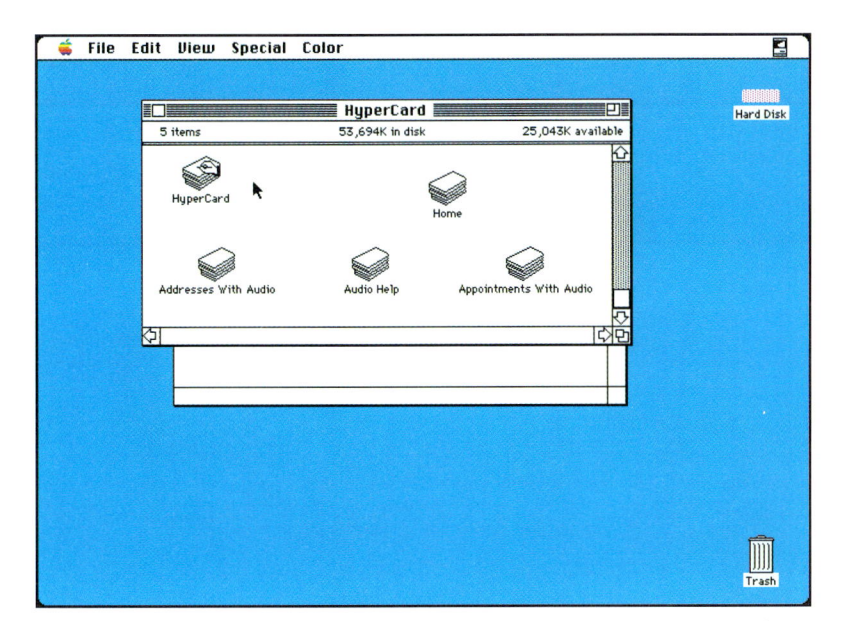

after

From the **File** menu, select **Quit HyperCard**.

> **Don't have HyperCard or the stacks?**
> If you don't have HyperCard or the stacks mentioned here, you cannot complete this or any of the other tasks in this section.

REVIEW

To quit HyperCard

TASK

Add a new address card

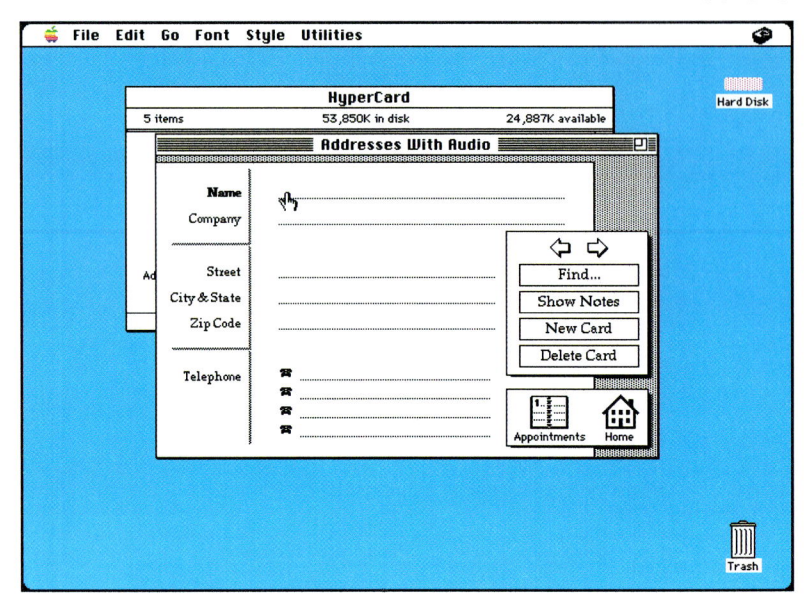

before

Oops!
If you decide you don't want the card, delete it. See *TASK: Delete an address card*.

1. Open the **Addresses With Audio** stack.

   This step opens the address stack and displays a sample address card. For help with this step, see *TASK: Open the Addresses With Audio stack*.

2. Click on **New Card**.

   This step selects the New Card button and displays a blank card. The Before screen shows this step.

3. In the Name field, type **Darlene Ball** and press **Tab**.

   This step enters the name for the address card and moves the insertion point to the Company field.

4. Type **Gerdt House** and press **Tab**.

   This step enters the name of the company and moves the insertion point to the Street field.

5. Type **1 Main Street** and press **Tab**.

   This step enters the address and moves the insertion point to the City and State field.

6. Type **Oldenburg, IN** and press **Tab**.

   This step enters the city and state and moves the insertion point to the ZIP Code field.

Easy **Macintosh**

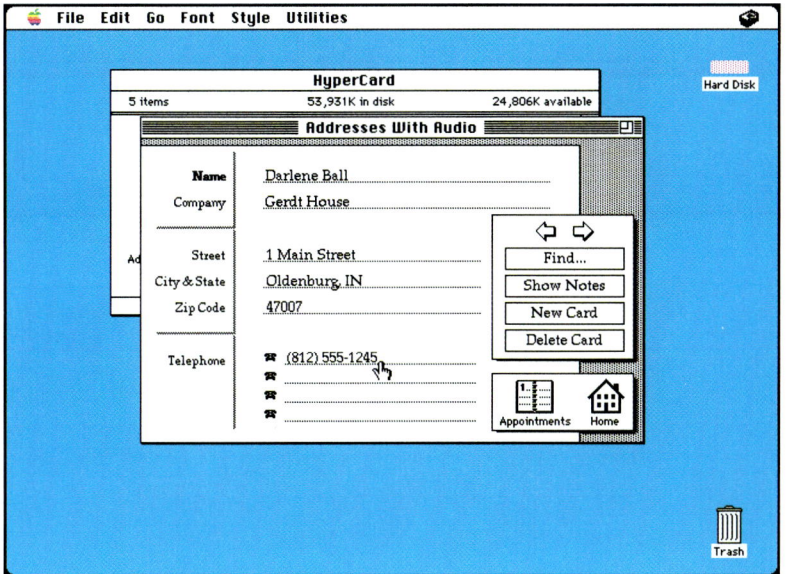

after

7. Type **47007** and press **Tab**.

   This step enters the ZIP code and moves the insertion point to the telephone field.

8. Type **(812) 555-1245**.

   This step enters the telephone number. The card is now complete.

Don't have HyperCard or the stacks?
If you don't have HyperCard or the stacks mentioned here, you cannot complete this or any of the other tasks in this section.

REVIEW

1. Open the **Addresses With Audio** stack.
2. Click on the **New Card** button.
3. Type the entries for those fields you want to complete.

To add a new address card

Working with HyperCard Stacks

155

TASK

Display a different address card

before

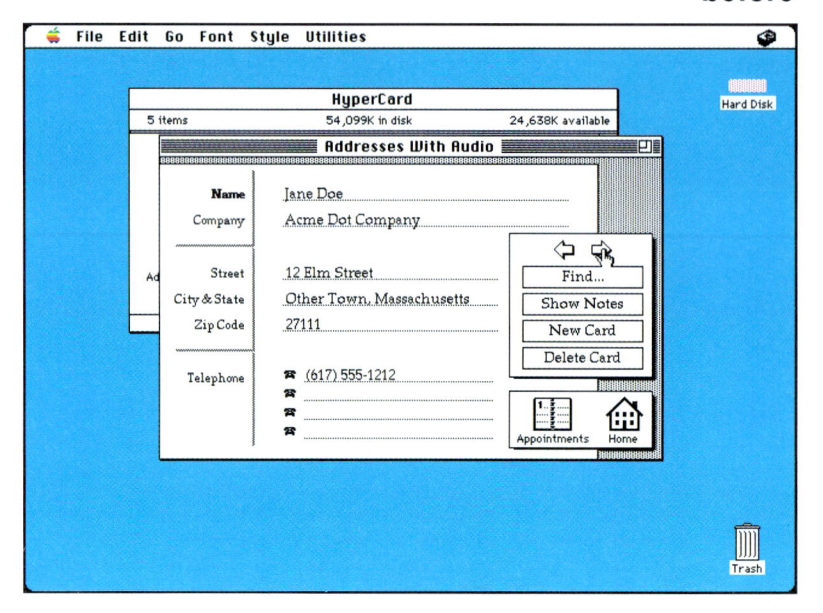

Oops!
If there is only one card, nothing happens when you click on the arrow button. You need to add more cards before you can display other cards.

1. Open the **Addresses With Audio** stack.

   This step opens the address stack and displays the first address card. For help with this step, see *TASK: Open the Addresses With Audio stack*.

2. Click on the → button.

   This step displays the next card in the stack.

156

Easy **Macintosh**

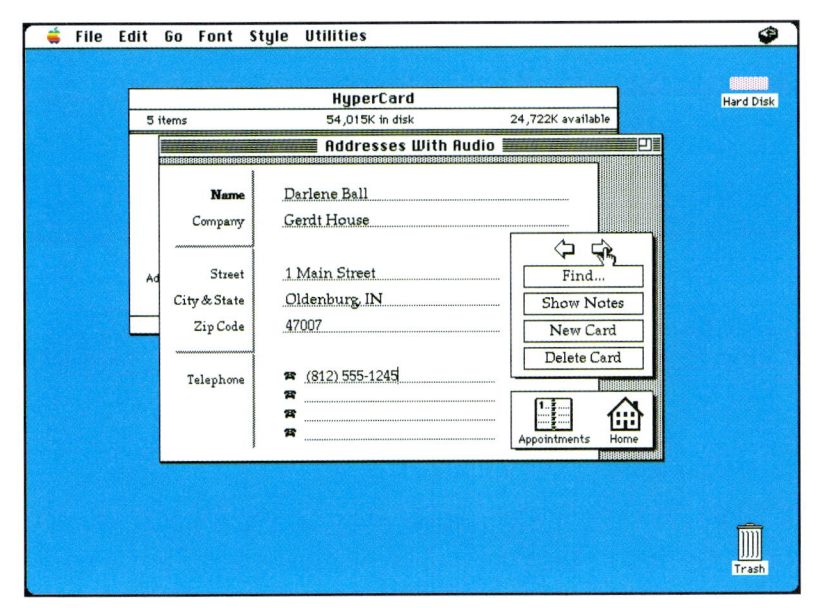

after

1. Open the **Addresses With Audio stack**.
2. Click on the → button to display the next card; click on the ← button to display the previous card.

Use the Find button
This method works well if you have just a few cards. If you have a lot of cards, use the Find button to move quickly to the card you want. See *TASK: Find an address card*.

REVIEW

To display a different address card

Don't have HyperCard or the stacks?
If you don't have HyperCard or the stacks mentioned here, you cannot complete this or any of the other tasks in this section.

Working with HyperCard Stacks

TASK

Find an address card

before

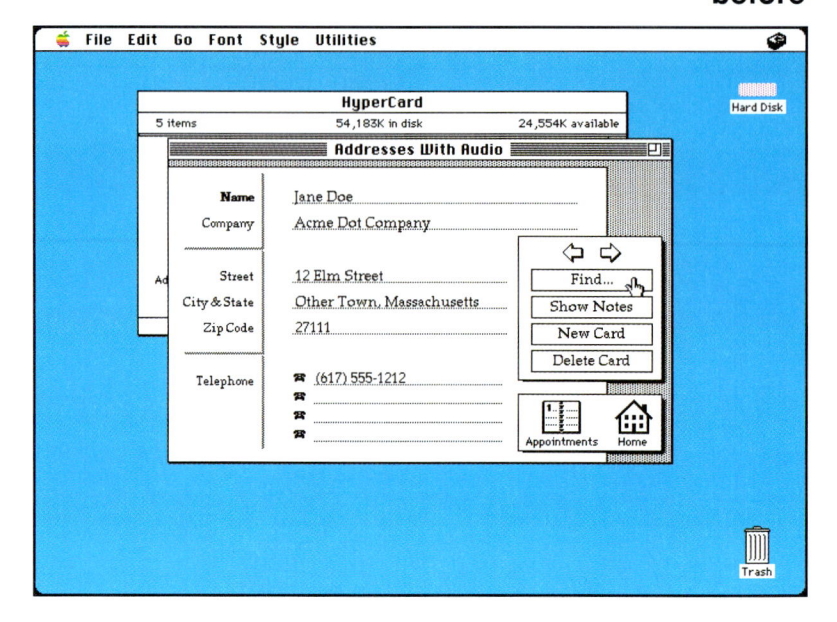

Oops!
If the selected text is not found, you hear the alert sound and a message box appears that states the text was not found. Click on the OK button and try the search again.

1. **Open the Addresses With Audio stack.**
   This step opens the address stack and displays the first address card. For help with this step, see *TASK: Open the Addresses With Audio stack*.

2. **Click on Find.**
   This step selects the Find button. You see a dialog box that prompts you `What text do you want to find?`

3. **Type Ball.**
   This step specifies the text you want to find. You can enter text that is in any field on the card.

4. **Click on OK.**
   Clicking on the OK button tells HyperCard to search the stack and display the first matching card. The text you entered in step 3 is boxed on the card.

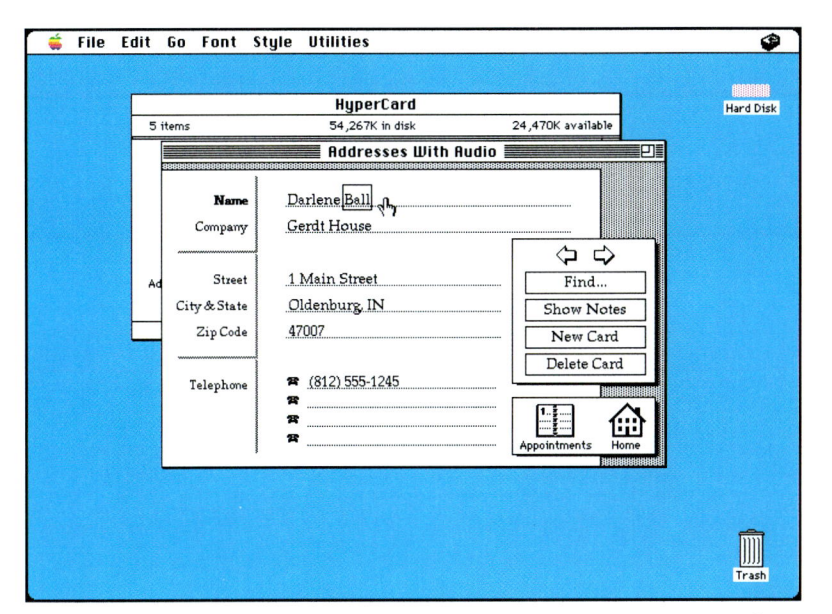

after

Don't have HyperCard or the stacks?
If you don't have HyperCard or the stacks mentioned here, you cannot complete this or any of the other tasks in this section.

REVIEW

1. Open the **Addresses With Audio stack**.
2. Click on the **Find** button.
3. Type the text you want to find.
4. Click on the **OK** button.

To find an address card

Working with HyperCard Stacks

159

TASK

Add a note to an address card

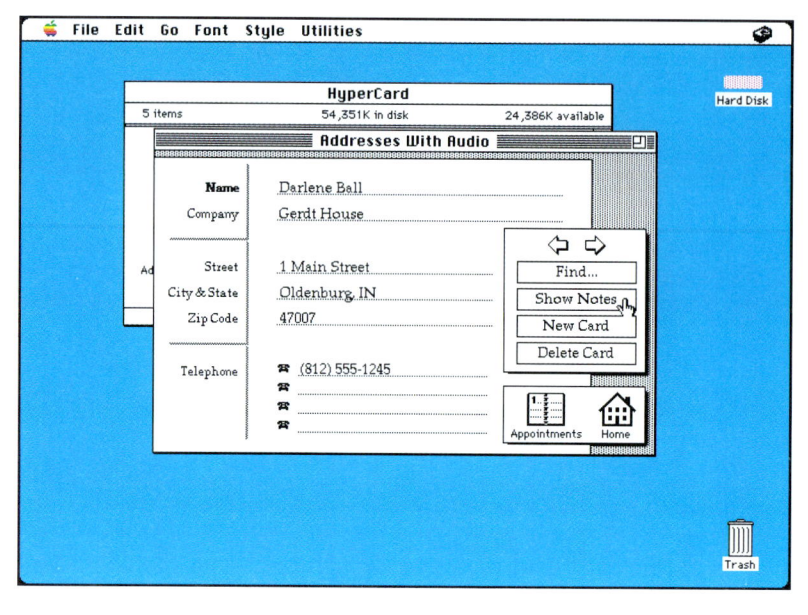

before

Oops!
To hide the notes, click on the Hide Notes button.

1. Open the **Addresses With Audio** stack.

   This step opens the address stack and displays the first address card. For help with this step, *see TASK: Open the Addresses With Audio stack*.

2. Click on the ➡ button until you see the card for Darlene Ball.

   For help with this step, see *TASK: Display a different address card*. The Before screen shows this step.

3. Click on **Show Notes**.

   This step selects the Show Notes button. You see a note box.

4. Click in the note box.

   This step places the insertion point in the note box so that you can type the note.

5. Type **Quilts, dolls, doll houses**.

   This step enters the note for the address card. The After screen shows this step.

160

Easy **Macintosh**

after

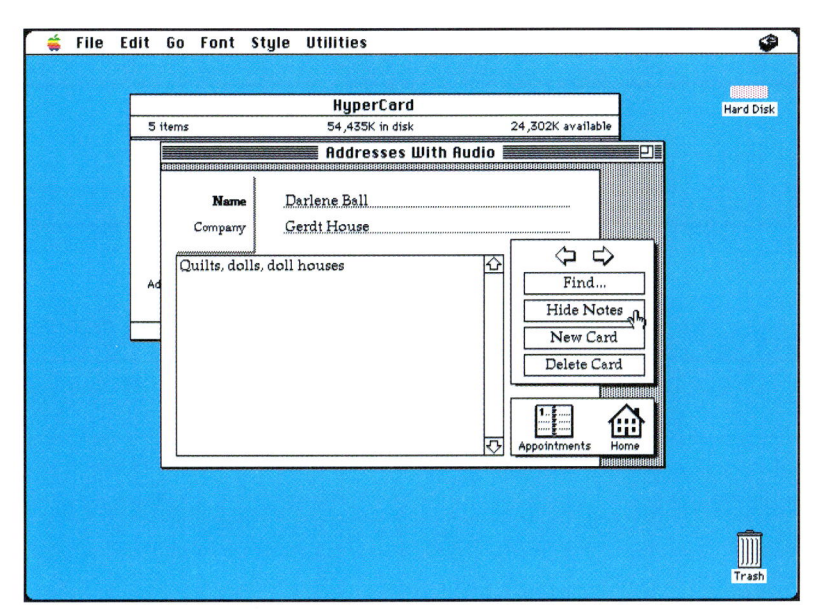

To display a note
Click on Show Notes to display the note you have entered.

REVIEW

1. Open the **Addresses With Audio** stack.
2. Display the card for which you want to add a note.
3. Click on the **Show Notes** button.
4. Click in the note box.
5. Type the note.

To add a note to an address card

Don't have HyperCard or the stacks?
If you don't have HyperCard or the stacks mentioned here, you cannot complete this or any of the other tasks in this section.

Working with HyperCard Stacks

161

TASK

Edit an address card

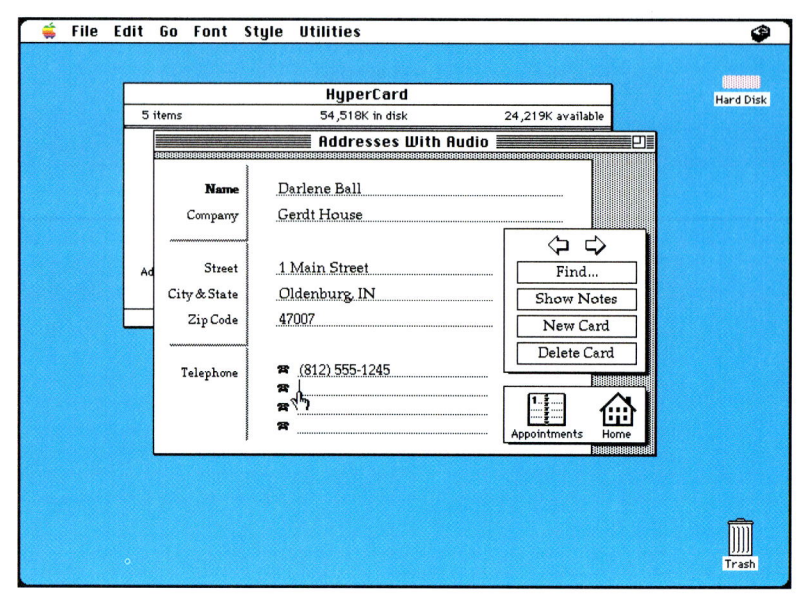

before

Oops!
If you change your mind about the addition, select the text you added and press the Delete key.

1. Open the **Addresses With Audio** stack.
   This step opens the address stack and displays the first address card. For help with this step, see *TASK: Open the Addresses With Audio stack*.

2. Click on the ➡ button until you see the card for Darlene Ball.
   For help with this step, see *TASK: Display a different address card*.

3. Click on the second line of the telephone field.
   This step moves the insertion point where you want to add text. The Before screen shows this step.

4. Type **(812) 555-3900 FAX**.
   This step adds a second phone number to the address card.

162

Easy **Macintosh**

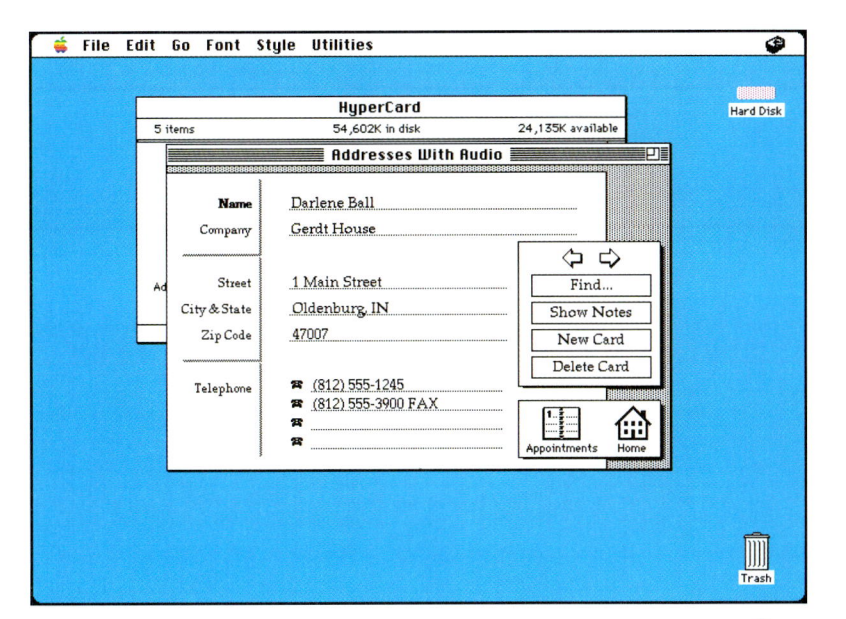

after

Don't have HyperCard or the stacks?
If you don't have HyperCard or the stacks mentioned here, you cannot complete this or any of the other tasks in this section.

REVIEW

1. Open the **Addresses With Audio** stack.
2. Display the card you want to edit.
3. Make any changes.

To edit an address card

Working with HyperCard Stacks

163

TASK

Delete an address card

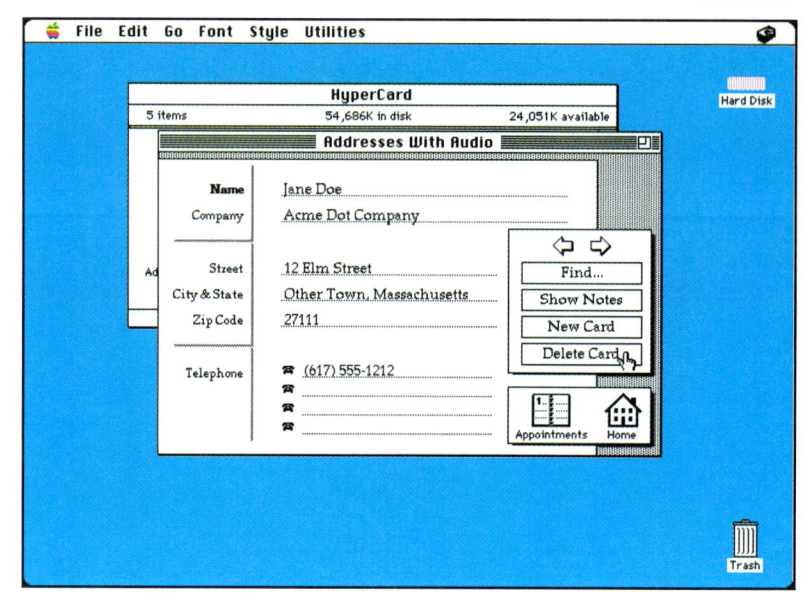

before

Oops!
If you change your mind, click on Cancel for step 4.

1. Open the **Addresses With Audio** stack.

   This step opens the address stack and displays the first address card. For help with this step, see *TASK: Open the Addresses With Audio stack*.

2. Be sure that the sample card is displayed.

   HyperCard includes a few sample cards. Display the one for Jane Doe.

3. Click on **Delete**.

   This step selects the Delete button. You see an alert box that asks `Delete this address card?`

4. Click on **OK**.

   Clicking on the OK button deletes the current card and displays the next card in the stack.

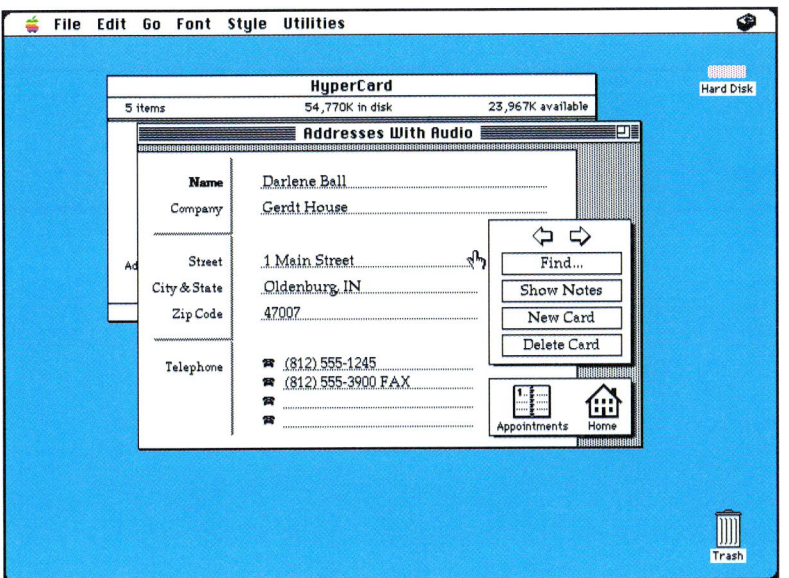

after

1. Open the **Addresses With Audio** stack.
2. Display the card you want to delete.
3. Click on the **Delete** button.
4. Click on the **OK** button.

Don't have HyperCard or the stacks?
If you don't have HyperCard or the stacks mentioned here, you cannot complete this or any of the other tasks in this section.

REVIEW

To delete an address card

Working with HyperCard Stacks

TASK

Open the Appointments With Audio stack

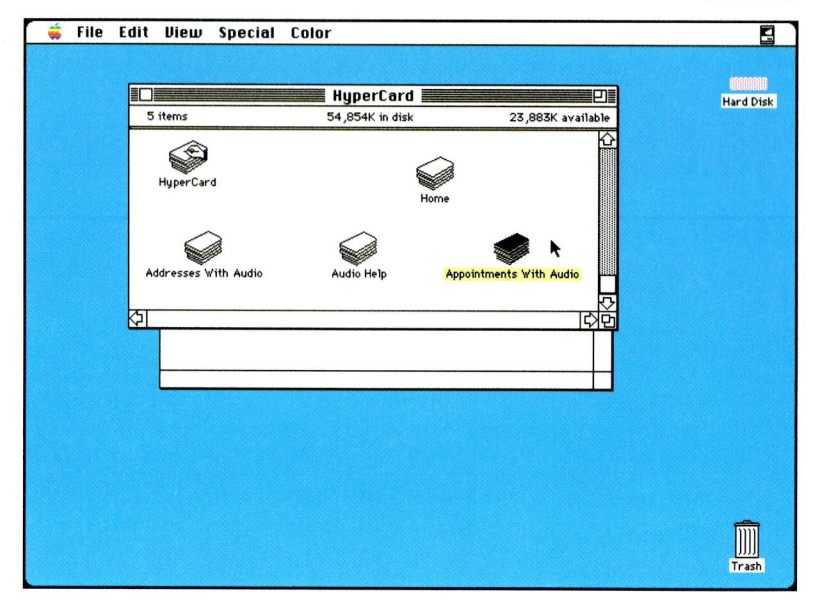

before

Oops!
To close the HyperCard stack, see *TASK: Quit HyperCard*.

1. Open the **HyperCard** folder.

   For help with this step, see *TASK: Open a folder*. You see a window displaying several different stacks. A HyperCard stack is a collection of cards.

2. Double-click on the **Appointments With Audio** icon.

   This step opens the Appointments With Audio stack. This HyperCard stack is supplied with the Macintosh. If you do not have this stack, skip this and all the other tasks in this section.

   You see a date calendar on the left side of the screen and a month calendar on the right. The current date appears in the date calendar and is boldfaced in the month calendar.

   Buttons appear to the right of the appointment card. These buttons let you find a card, add notes, and move among cards. (See the other tasks in this section.)

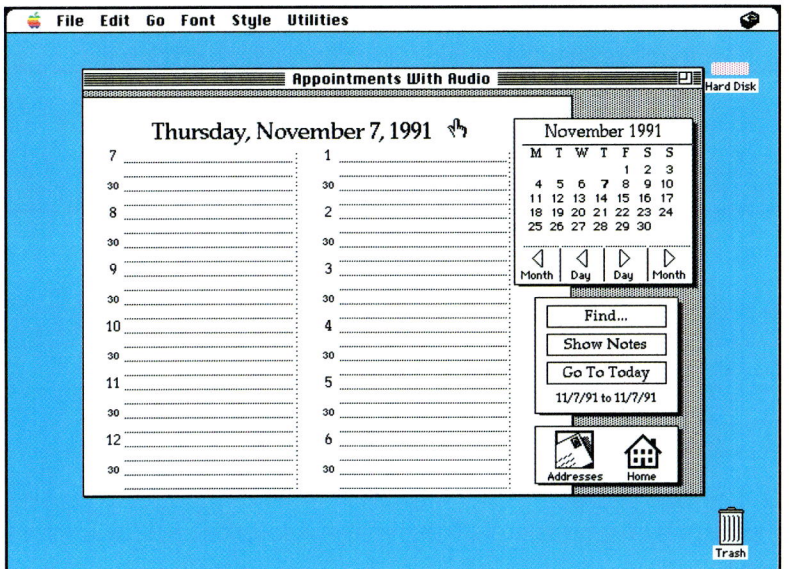

after

1. Open the **HyperCard** folder.

2. Double-click on the **Appointments With Audio** icon.

Don't have HyperCard or the stacks?
If you don't have HyperCard or the stacks mentioned here, you cannot complete this or any of the other tasks in this section.

REVIEW

To open the Appointments With Audio stack

What is HyperCard?
HyperCard is a complete application with its own menu system. For help with all HyperCard tasks, see Que's *HyperCard 2 QuickStart*.

Working with HyperCard Stacks

167

TASK

Display a different appointment date

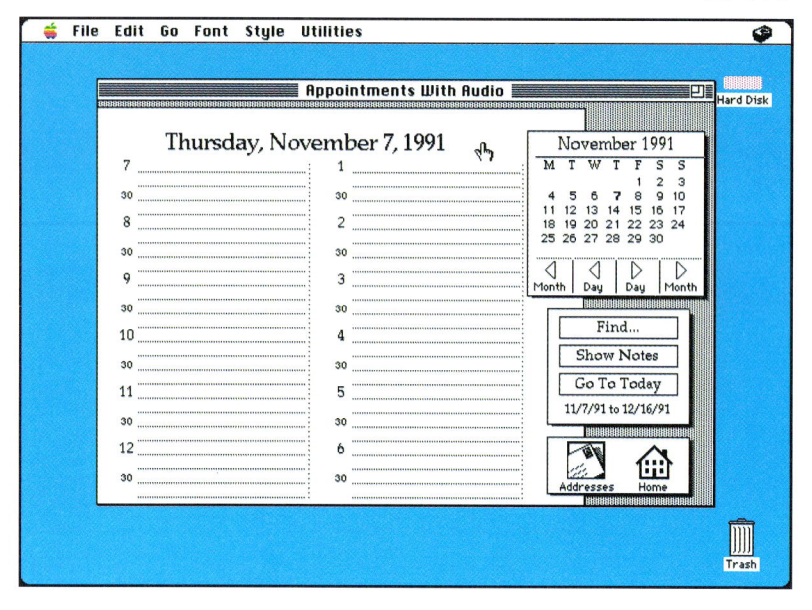

before

Oops!
Click on the Go To Today button to return to the current date.

1. Open the **Appointments With Audio** stack.

   This step opens the appointment stack and displays the current date. For help with this step, see *TASK: Open the Appointments With Audio stack*.

2. Click on the ▷**Month** button.

   This step displays the next month in the month calendar. (In the Before screen, the next month is December.)

   You might see a note that states that no cards exist for this date. If so, click on the OK button.

3. Double-click on **14** in the calendar area.

   This step selects December 14 as the date. This date appears in the date calendar.

   You might see a note that states that no cards exist for this month. If so, click on the OK button.

   You also can click on the ▷Day button to move to this date, but double-clicking on the date is quicker.

Easy **Macintosh**

after

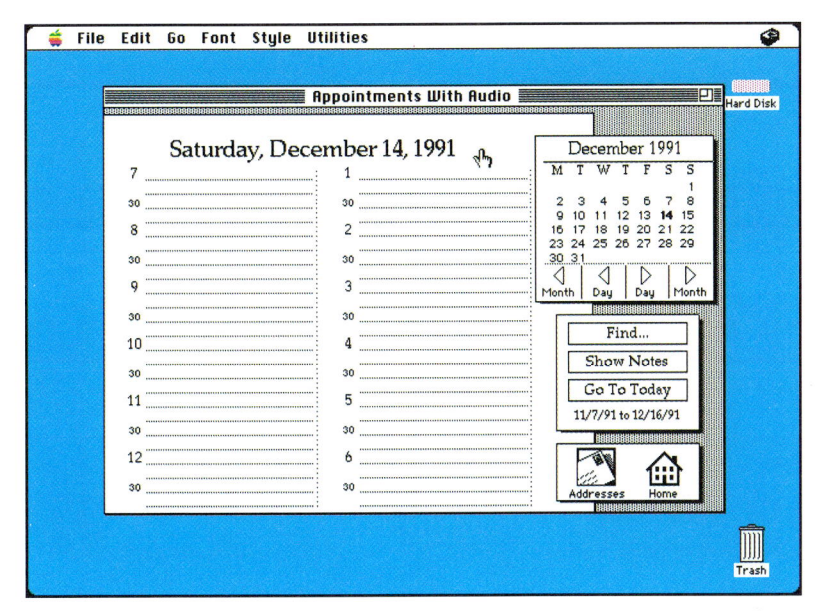

Don't have HyperCard or the stacks?
If you don't have HyperCard or the stacks mentioned here, you cannot complete this or any of the other tasks in this section.

REVIEW

1. Open the **Appointments With Audio** stack.

2. Click on the ▷ or ◁ **Day** or **Month** buttons to display the date you want.

To display a different appointment date

Working with HyperCard Stacks

169

TASK

Add an appointment

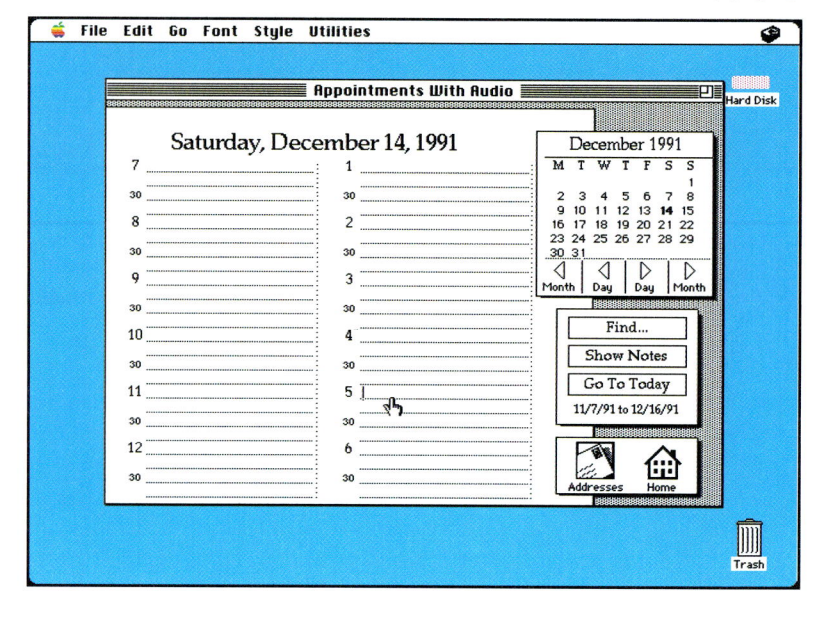

before

Oops!
To delete an appointment, see TASK: Delete an appointment.

1. Open the **Appointments With Audio** stack.
   This step opens the address stack and displays the current date. For help with this step, see TASK: Open the Appointments With Audio stack.

2. Display the date **December 14, 1991**.
   For help with this step, see TASK: Display a different appointment date. The Before screen shows this step.

3. In the date book area, click next to **5**.
   This step selects the time—5 PM—for the appointment.

4. Type **Company Christmas party** and press **Return**.
   This step enters the first line of the appointment entry.

5. Type **Hyatt Regency**.
   This step enters the second line of the appointment entry.

Easy **Macintosh**

after

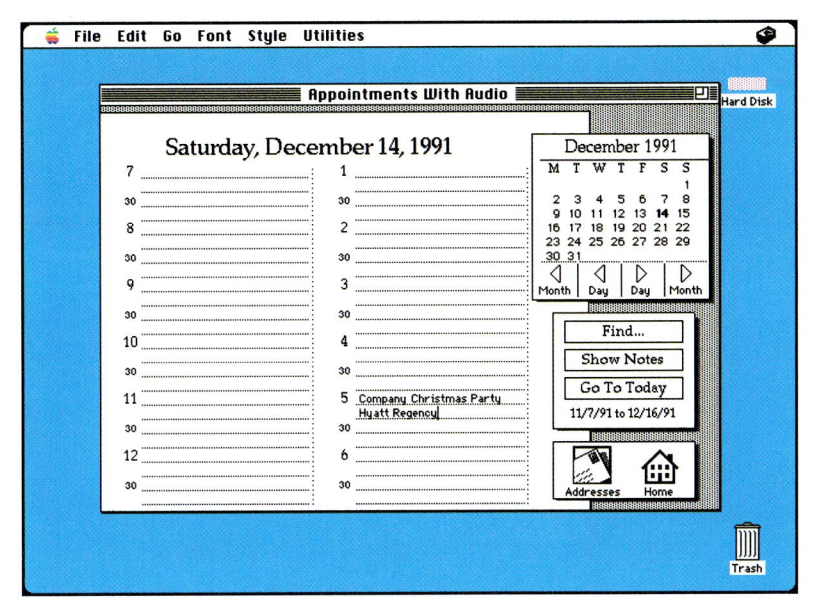

Don't have HyperCard or the stacks?
If you don't have HyperCard or the stacks mentioned here, you cannot complete this or any of the other tasks in this section.

REVIEW

1. Open the **Appointments With Audio** stack.

2. Display the date on which you want to enter an appointment.

3. Click next to the time for the appointment.

4. Type the appointment.

To add an appointment

TASK

Find an appointment card

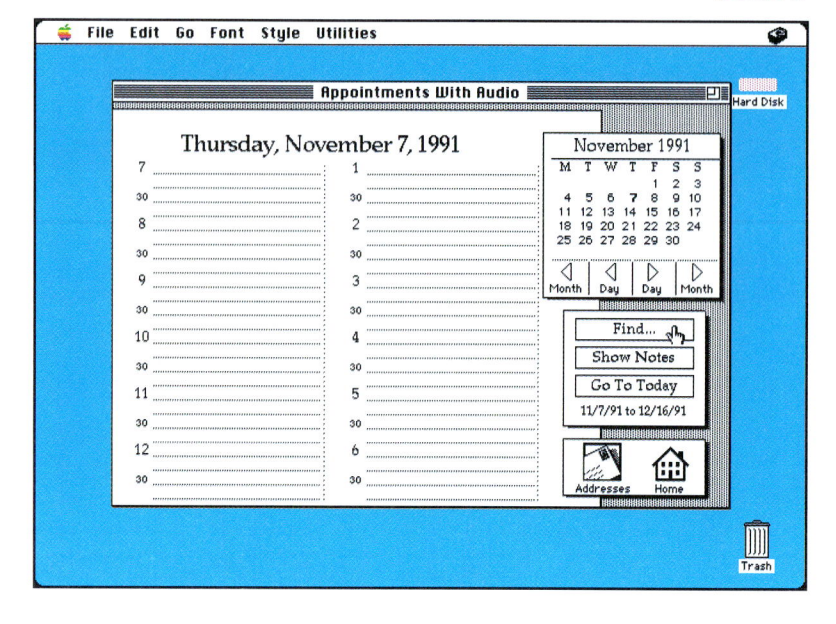

before

Oops!
If the selected text is not found, you hear the alert sound and a message box appears to state that the text was not found. Click on the OK button and try the search again.

1. Open the **Appointments With Audio** stack.

   This step opens the address stack and displays the current date. For help with this step, see *TASK: Open the Appointments With Audio stack*.

2. Click on **Find**.

   This step selects the Find button. You see a dialog box that asks `What text do you want to find?`

3. Type **Christmas**.

   This step specifies the text that you want to find. You can enter text that is in any field on the card.

4. Click on **OK**.

   Clicking on the OK button tells HyperCard to search the stack and display the first matching card. The text you entered in step 3 is boxed on the card.

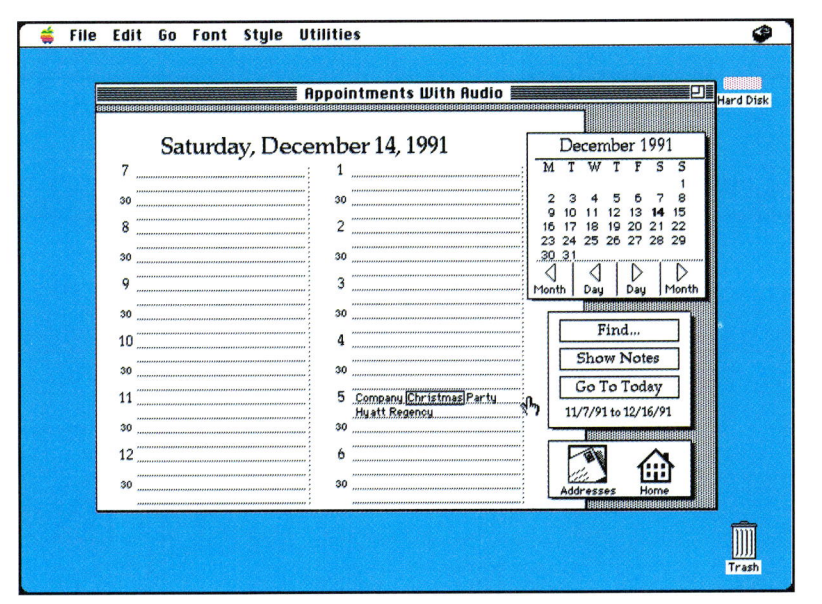

after

1. Open the **Appointments With Audio** stack.
2. Click on the **Find** button.
3. Type the text you want to find.
4. Click on **OK**.

Don't have HyperCard or the stacks?
If you don't have HyperCard or the stacks mentioned here, you cannot complete this or any of the other tasks in this section.

REVIEW

To find an appointment card

Working with HyperCard Stacks

TASK

Add a note to an appointment card

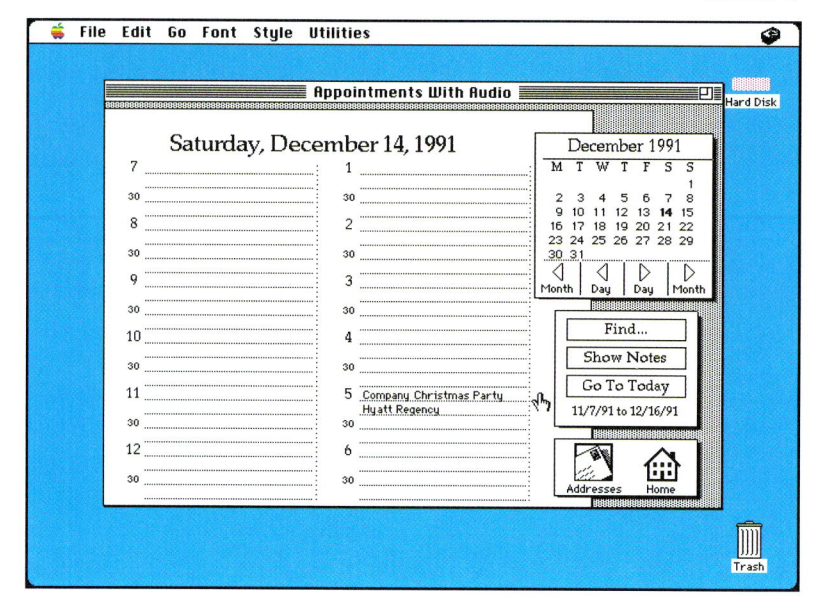

before

Oops!
To hide the notes, click on the Hide Notes button.

1. Open the **Appointments With Audio** stack.

   This step opens the address stack and displays the current date. For help with this step, see *TASK: Open the Appointments With Audio stack*.

2. Display the date **December 14, 1991**.

   For help with this step, see *TASK: Display a different appointment date*. The Before screen shows this step.

3. Click on the **Show Notes** button.

   This step selects the Show Notes button. You see a note box.

4. Type **Black Tie**.

   This step enters the note for the card. The After screen shows this step.

174

Easy Macintosh

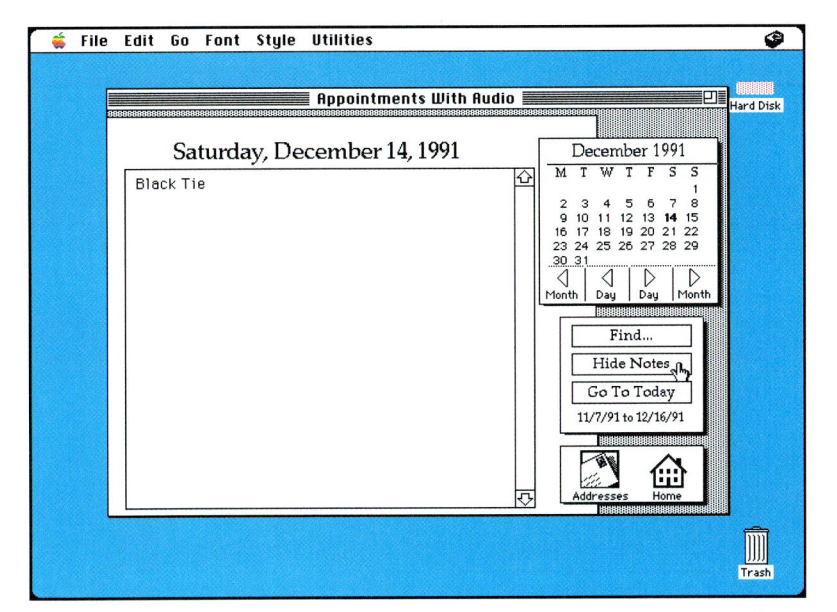

To display a note
Click on Show Notes to display the note you have entered.

after

REVIEW

1. Open the **Appointments With Audio stack**.
2. Display the card for which you want to add a note.
3. Click on the **Show Notes** button.
4. Type the note.

To add a note to an appointment card

Don't have HyperCard or the stacks?
If you don't have HyperCard or the stacks mentioned here, you cannot complete this or any of the other tasks in this section.

Working with HyperCard Stacks

175

TASK

Edit an appointment card

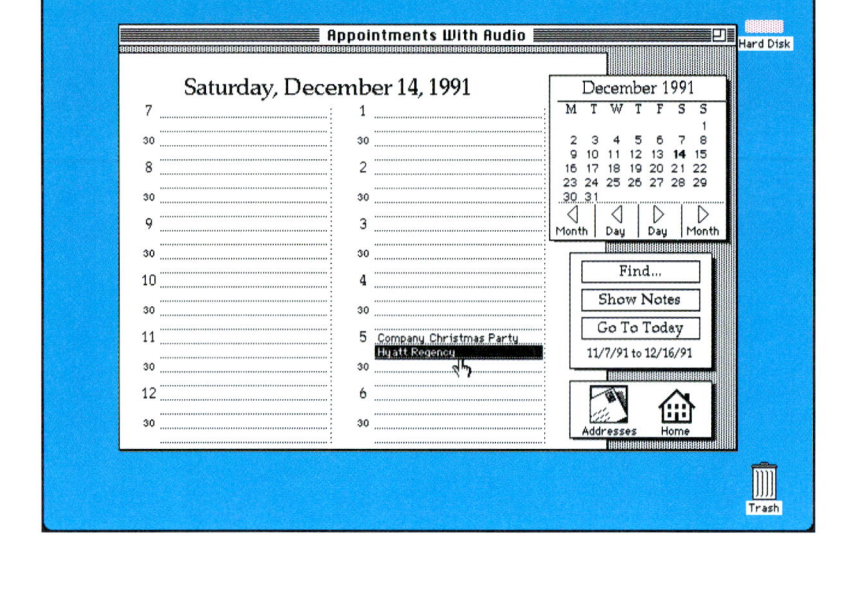

before

Oops!
If you change your mind, select Undo from the Edit menu.

1. Open the **Appointments With Audio** stack.

   This step opens the address stack and displays the current date. For help with this step, see *TASK: Open the Appointments With Audio stack*.

2. Display the date **December 14, 1991**.

   For help with this step, see *TASK: Display a different appointment date*.

3. Click before *Hyatt Regency* on the second line of the appointment entry.

   This step moves the insertion point to where you want to change text.

4. Click and hold down the mouse button; drag across the text **Hyatt Regency**.

   This step selects the text you want to replace. The text appears in reverse video. The Before screen shows this step.

5. Type **Hilton**.

   The new text replaces the selected text.

Easy **Macintosh**

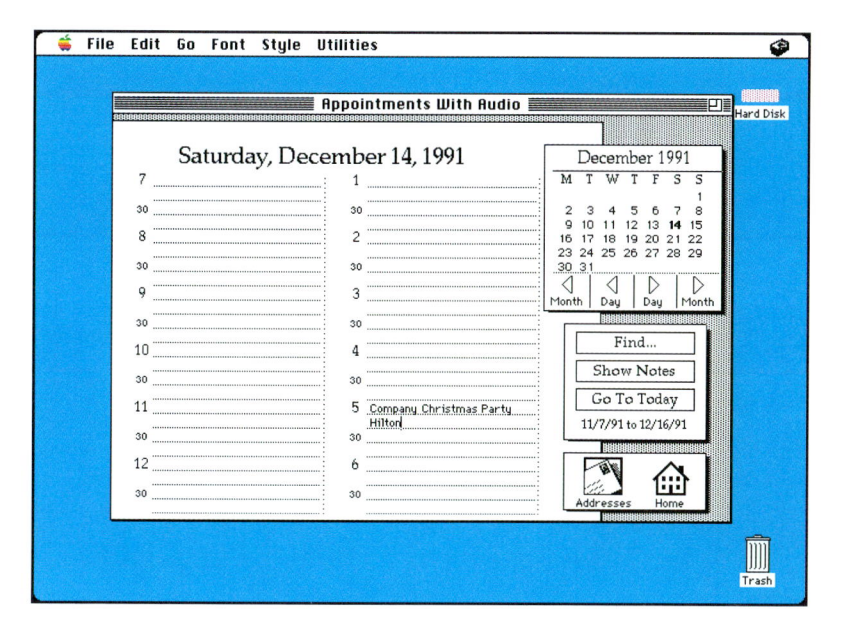

after

Don't have HyperCard or the stacks?
If you don't have HyperCard or the stacks mentioned here, you cannot complete this or any of the other tasks in this section.

REVIEW

1. Open the **Appointments With Audio** stack.
2. Display the card you want to edit.
3. Make any changes.

To edit an appointment card

Working with HyperCard Stacks

177

TASK

Delete an appointment

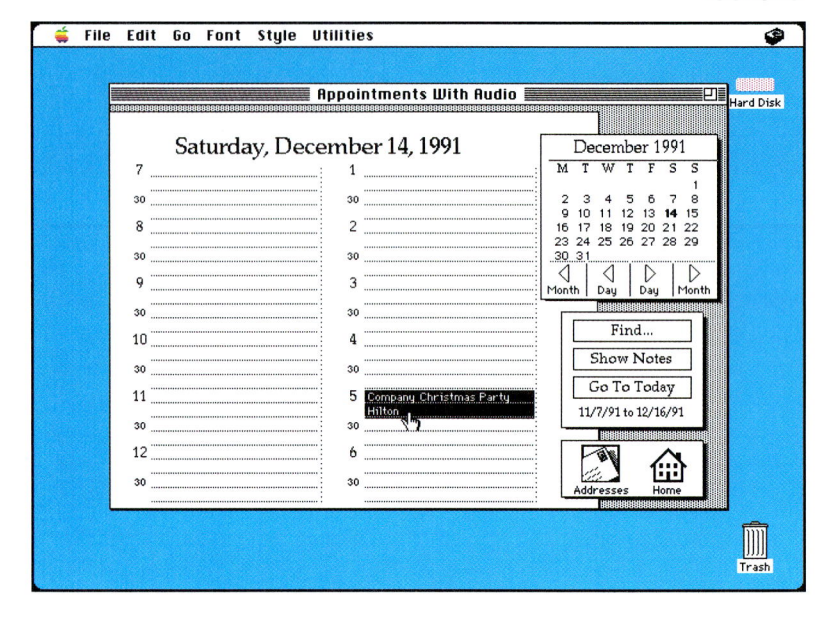

before

Oops!
If you change your mind, select Undo from the Edit menu.

1. Open the **Appointments With Audio** stack.

   This step opens the appointment stack and displays the appointment card for the current date. For help with this step, see *TASK: Open the Appointments With Audio stack*.

2. Display the date **December 14, 1991**.

   For help with this step, see *TASK: Display a different appointment date*.

3. Click before the *C* in *Company*.

   This step moves the insertion point to where you want to delete text.

4. Click and hold down the mouse button; drag across the text to select both lines of the appointment entry.

   This step selects the text you want to delete. The text appears in reverse video. The Before screen shows this step.

5. Press **Delete**.

   Pressing the Delete key deletes the appointment entry. Keep in mind that the actual appointment card is the date—you don't want to delete the card, you want to delete the appointment entry. Deleting the card is similar to tearing a page out of a date book. Deleting an entry is similar to erasing the entry from the date book.

Easy **Macintosh**

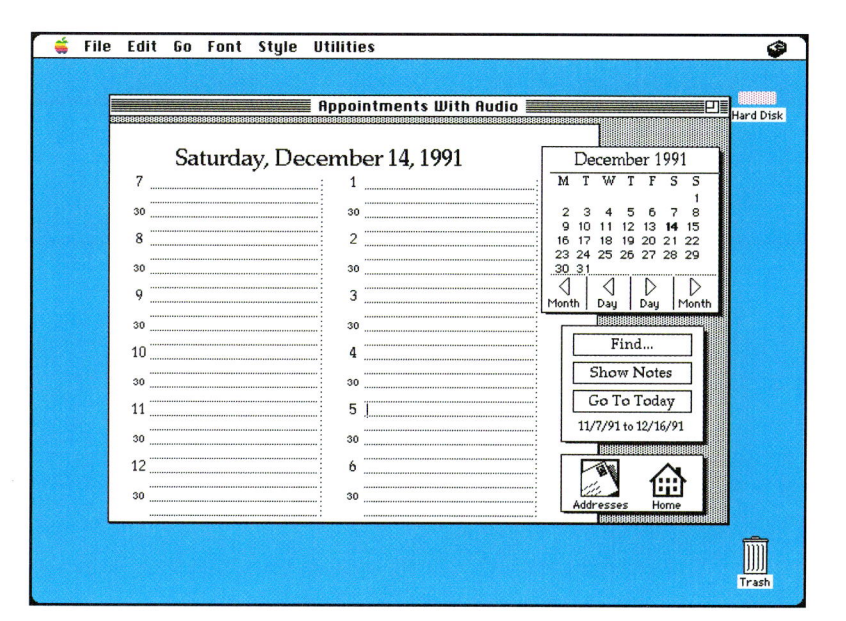

after

1. Open the **Appointments With Audio** stack.
2. Display the entry you want to delete.
3. Select the text for the appointment entry.
4. Press the **Delete** key.

Don't have HyperCard or the stacks?
If you don't have HyperCard or the stacks mentioned here, you cannot complete this or any of the other tasks in this section.

REVIEW

To delete an appointment

Reference

Quick Reference

Software Guide

Glossary

Easy Macintosh

Reference

Quick Reference Guide

Task	Command	Shortcut Keys
Arrange icons	**Special**, **Clean Up Window**	
Create a new folder	**File**, **New Folder**	⌘-N
Close a window	**File**, **Close** or click on the **close box**	⌘-W
Change alert sound	, **Control Panel** (Sound)	
Change date	, **Control Panel** (General)	
Change Desktop	, **Control Panel** (General)	
Change time	, **Control Panel** (General)	
Change speaker volume	, **Control Panel** (General)	
Duplicate a file	**File**, **Duplicate**	⌘-D
Display information about an icon	**File**, **Get Info**	
Display special characters	, **Key Caps**	
Display time	, **Alarm Clock**	
Eject a disk	**File**, **Eject** or drag disk to the **Trash can** icon	⌘-E
Empty trash	**Special**, **Empty Trash**	
Erase disk	**Special**, **Erase Disk**	
Find file	, **Find File**	
Open an icon	**File**, **Open** or double-click on the icon	⌘-O
Shut down the Macintosh	**Special**, **Shut Down**	

182

Easy **Macintosh**

Task	Command	Shortcut Keys
Use calculator	**, Calculator**	
View small icons	**View, by Small Icon**	
View icons	**View, by Icon**	
View names	**View, by Name**	
View dates	**View, by Date**	
View size	**View, by Size**	
View kind	**View, by Kind**	

Software Guide

To use your Macintosh to perform a specific task (writing a letter, balancing a budget, storing real estate clients), you need to purchase and install applications. Applications are tools you use on the Macintosh.

This guide discusses the most common categories of applications, briefly explains the function of each type, and lists a few representative software packages. For more information, see *The Big Mac Book,* 2nd Edition, or pick up a Macintosh magazine, such as *MacUser* or *MACWORLD*, and read the articles and advertisements.

Types of Applications

There are basically 10 categories of applications:

- Word processors
- Spreadsheets
- Databases
- Graphics
- Desktop publishing
- Communication
- Integrated programs
- Financial
- Education
- Games

In addition, you might want to add desk accessories (mini-applications) and utilities. The following sections discuss each type of program.

Word Processors

You use word processors to create memos, letters, reports, brochures, and other printed material. A word processor is like a typewriter—but much better.

Most word processors offer several features that make it easy to work with text. You can

See text on-screen as you type.   Because the text is not committed to paper, you can make changes and corrections—delete text, add text, and so on.

Rearrange text.   As you write, you might decide that the last paragraph really belongs in the introduction. With a word processor, you can move the text from one spot to another. This process is called *cut and paste*.

Spell check your document.   Nothing mars a document worse than a glaring typo or misspelled word. Most word processors offer a speller. You can check the spelling of your document before you print.

Save a document.   You can save the document on disk and use it again.

Format a document.   Word processors vary in the formatting features they offer. Simple word processors enable you to set tabs, change margins, select different fonts or font styles (bold, italic, and so on). Complex word processors include these features, and they also allow you to add footers and headers, create columns, insert graphics, and so on.

The most common word processing programs are

- MacWrite II
- Nisus
- Word for the Macintosh
- WordPerfect

Spreadsheets

A spreadsheet is an electronic version of an accountant's pad. You use a spreadsheet program to set up worksheets. Worksheets can total sales by division, keep track of a monthly budget, figure loan balances, and perform other financial analyses.

With a spreadsheet program, you can

Calculate formulas. You can write simple formulas to add, subtract, multiply, and divide. You can depend on the spreadsheet program to calculate the results correctly every time.

Change data and recalculate. When you change, add, or delete data, the spreadsheet recalculates the results automatically. You don't have to erase and rewrite when you forget a crucial figure. And you don't have to refigure all the amounts manually when you make a change or an addition.

Rearrange data. With your worksheet on-screen, you can add or delete a column or row. You can copy and move data from one spot to another.

Repeat information. You can copy text, a value, or a formula from one place to another in the worksheet. In your monthly budget worksheet, for example, you total the expenses for each month. You could write a formula that calculates January totals, and then copy this formula for February through December.

Change the format of data. You can format your results in many ways. You can display a number with dollar signs, as a percent, or as a date. You can align text left, right, or center.

Print data. You can print reports of your data.

Create graphs. Most spreadsheet programs enable you to graph your data and print that graph. You can create pie graphs, bar graphs, line graphs, and many other graph types.

The most common spreadsheet programs are

- Full Impact
- Lotus 1-2-3 for the Macintosh
- Microsoft Excel for the Macintosh
- Resolve
- Wingz

Databases

A database is similar to a complex card file. You store related information together. You can use a database to keep track of real estate clients, a baseball card collection, employees, inventory—any set of data.

Each piece of data—for example, a phone number—is stored in a *field*. A set of fields — such as a name field, an address field, and a phone number field—make up a *record*. A *database* is a collection of all the records.

Databases enable you to

Retrieve data.   After you enter data, you can easily retrieve it. Rather than sift through several paper documents, you can quickly pull up an invoice on-screen, for example.

Sort data.   You can rearrange data. For instance, you might want an alphabetical list of clients, sorted by last name, to use as a phone list. You might want to sort the same list by ZIP code to do a mailing.

Print data.   You can print reports, mailing labels, and other output.

Some of the most common database packages include

- 4th Dimension
- FileMaker Pro
- FoxBase+/Mac

Graphics

With graphics programs, you can create simple to complex illustrations. This category also includes presentation programs, which enable you to create graphs, and computer-aided design programs (CAD), which enable you to create architectural and other complex drawings.

Graphics programs offer these advantages:

Provide many drawing tools. Different packages offer different drawing tools. These tools can enable you to draw geometric shapes (circles, squares, rectangles, lines, and so on), add fills and color, add text, trace objects, align objects, and so on.

Edit drawings. If you don't get the drawing just right, you can modify it. You can delete and redraw parts of the drawing.

Create drawings to be used over and over. You might, for instance, create a logo that you could use for letterhead, business cards, and so on.

Programs in this category include

- Adobe Illustrator (draw)
- Aldus Freehand (draw)
- Aldus Persuasion (graph)
- Aldus SuperPaint (paint and draw)
- CA-Cricket Graph (graph)
- Canvas(paint)
- Claris CAD (CAD)
- MacDraw Pro (draw)
- MacPaint (paint)

Desktop Publishing

Desktop publishing programs enable you to create sophisticated brochures, newsletters, fliers, resumes, invitations, menus, reports, and other output. Some word processing packages offer desktop publishing capabilities (such as column layout), but the features offered by desktop publishing programs are more sophisticated. Keep in mind that if you do use a desktop publishing program, you will probably use a word processor to create the text.

A desktop publishing program offers these features:

Layout a page.   With a desktop publishing program, you have precise control over the layout of the page—the margins, headers, footers, and so on. You also have control over the text—what font, size, and style are used; where the text is placed; and how the text flows.

Change page layout.   If you don't like the way the document looks, you can change the document. You can experiment with the layout until you get the document just the way you want it.

Create templates.   You can create a template for the type of document that you use over and over, such as a newsletter. The headings and layout would be set—you just have to add the text.

The most popular desktop publishing packages are

- Aldus PageMaker
- QuarkXPress
- Ready, Set, Go!
- Ventura Publisher

Communication

Communication programs enable you to use your computer to talk to other computers. You might, for example, need to access a huge computer (called a *mainframe*) that stores stock figures so that you can get up-to-the-minute reports. Or you might need some sales data from your district office's computer. With a communication program, you can send and receive information over the phone lines.

To use your Macintosh to communicate, you also must have a modem, a phone line, and a communication package. MicroPhone and White Knight are examples of this type of package. (For more information on modems, see *Introduction to PCs*, 2nd Edition, or *The Big Mac Book*, 2nd Edition.)

Integrated Programs

Integrated programs combine several types of programs into one package: word processing, database, spreadsheet, and communications. Each of these programs offer the benefits previously discussed. They also have the added benefit of enabling you to integrate the data from one program into the next easily. You can use the mailing list from your database, for instance, to create form letters with your word processor. You can copy financial figures from the spreadsheet to a report in the word processor. On the down side, integrated packages do not offer as many features as stand-alone or dedicated packages.

Integrated packages include

- Microsoft Works
- ClarisWorks
- Greatworks
- BeagleWorks

Financial Programs

Financial programs enable you to create tax returns, balance your checkbook, set up an accounting system, and perform other finance-related tasks. These programs range from the simple to the complex. Some examples follow:

- CheckFree (simple electronic bill-paying utility)
- M.Y.O.B. (complete accounting package—general ledger, accounts receivable, accounts payable, payroll)
- MacIn Tax (tax preparation program)

- Managing Your Money (finance management package)
- Quicken (simple check-writing program—also can be used for limited accounting purposes)
- Wealthbuilder (financial investment advisor and manager—can also read information from Quicken and Managing Your Money)

Education

The Macintosh is easy to use, which makes it ideal for learning new tasks. You can use programs to learn how to type, read, or write a story. These programs are helpful for children and adults alike.

Some sample programs include

- Dinosaur Days
- KidPix
- Mavis Beacon Teaches Typing
- New Math Blaster Plus
- Reader Rabbit

Games

And last but not least, you can use the Macintosh to play games. Available games include

- Puzzle Master
- Swamp Gas
- Talking Moose
- Where in the USA is Carmen Sandiego?
- Wordtris

Desk Accessories and Utilities

Your Macintosh comes with a set of desk accessories (DAs). (Some of these are covered in the Task/Review part of this book.)

You also can add other desk accessories. AfterDark, for example, is a screen saver program that displays a picture on-screen if you haven't used the computer in a certain amount of time. Another DA, CanOpener, enables you to access any Macintosh document—no matter what program created it.

Utility programs help you manage your system better. You might want a program to undelete files, for example, or optimize your hard disk, compress files, check for viruses, or search files. Some utilities function as DAs; others are separate programs. Available desk accessories and utility programs include

- Checklist
- Heapfixer
- MacLink Plus/PC
- MacTools Deluxe

Others

Not all programs fit into a neat category. New programs are created every day. Programs are available that enable you to draw up a will, create a calendar, or perform complex statistical analyses. Just peruse some of the Macintosh magazines to get an idea of the world of possibilities. Explore with your Macintosh. Be productive. But most of all, have fun.

Glossary

application   A computer program used for a particular task—such as word processing. In most cases, the terms *program* and *application* mean the same thing and can be used interchangeably.

byte   A measure of an amount of information that is equal to about one character.

capacity   A term used to describe how much data you can store on a disk. Capacity is measured in kilobytes (K) or megabytes (M).

Chooser   A desk accessory that enables you to select a printer. Applications use the printer you have selected with the Chooser to print documents.

click   The action of pressing and releasing the mouse button once.

clipboard   A temporary spot in memory that holds text or graphics you cut or copy. This area is cleared after you turn off the Macintosh.

close box   A small box in the upper left corner of a window. Click on this box to close the window.

control panel   A desk accessory that enables you to customize features, such as the Desktop pattern, the alert sound, and the speaker volume.

desk accessory (DA)   A small application that performs a limited task (alarm clock, calculator, puzzle). Desk accessories are listed in the Apple menu. Some desk accessories come with the Macintosh.

Desktop   The work area of the Macintosh.

dialog box   An on-screen window that displays further command options. Many times a dialog box reminds you of the consequences or results of a command and asks you to confirm that you want to continue with the action.

document   A generic term used to describe text files created with applications. A document can be a letter, a picture, a worksheet, and so on.

double-click The action of pressing the mouse button twice in rapid succession.

drag The action of pointing to an item, and then pressing and holding down the left mouse button as you move the mouse.

file The various individual reports, memos, databases, and letters that you store on your hard drive (or disk) for future use. (Also called a *document*.)

Finder The part of the Macintosh operating system that keeps the Desktop organized.

floppy disk A storage device. Floppy disk drives read from and write to floppy disks.

floppy disk drive A storage device. Floppy disks are 3 1/2 inches; the floppy part is inside the plastic encasement.

folder An item on the Desktop that stores icons. A folder can contain files, other folders, or other types of information.

hardware The physical parts of the Macintosh—the screen, the keyboard, the mouse, and so on.

icon A picture that represents a file, folder, or application program.

initialize The process that prepares a disk for use.

kilobyte Approximately one thousand bytes (1024 to be exact). A kilobyte is a measurement used for files.

megabyte One million bytes of information.

menu An on-screen list of commands or options.

menu bar A list of menu names that appears near the top of the Desktop.

monitor   The piece of hardware that displays on-screen what you type on the keyboard.

program   A set of instructions that tells a computer what to do. (Same as *application*.)

scroll bars   The bars at the bottom and right of a window. At the ends of the bars are scroll arrows; click on an arrow to scroll the window in the direction of the arrow.

shut down   The action of saving all work, closing all applications, and turning off the computer.

size box   The box located in the lower right corner of a window. This size box enables you to resize the window.

software   Another term for computer programs or applications. You run software on your hardware.

System Folder   The folder that contains files necessary to start and use the Macintosh.

title bar   The horizontal bar at the top of a window. The title bar contains the name of the window.

Trash can icon   An icon used to delete files, folders, and applications.

window   A rectangular area on-screen in which you view an application or a document.

zoom box   The box located in the upper right corner of a window. The zoom box enables you to enlarge (zoom) the window.

Index

Easy WordPerfect

Index

A

adding
    addresses with Audio stack, 154-155
    appointment dates with Audio stack, 170-171
    notes to
        addresses with Audio stack, 160-161
        appointments with Audio stack, 174-175
addresses
    adding new, 154-155
    notes, 160-161
    deleting, 164-165
    displaying, 156-157
    editing, 162-163
    finding, 158-159
    opening, 150-151
Addresses with Audio icon (HyperCard folder), 150-151, 154-165
alarm, setting the, 142-143
Alarm Clock commands (Apple menu), 140-143
alert sound, changing, 138-139
Apple menu
    Alarm Clock command, 140-143
    Calculator command, 144-145
    Control Panel command, 130-139
    Find File command, 126-127
    Key Caps command, 146-147
applications, 2, 23, 30, 183-191
    deleting, 103
appointments
    adding, 170-171
        notes, 174-175
    deleting, 178-179
    displaying dates, 168-169
    editing, 176-177
    finding, 172-173
    opening, 166-167
Appointments with Audio icon (HyperCard folder), 166-179
arranging icons, 74-75
arrow keys, 19, 21
Audio Stack
    adding
        addresses, 154-155
        appointment dates, 170-171
        notes, 160-161, 174-175
    deleting
        addresses, 164-165
        appointments, 178-179
    displaying
        addresses, 156-157
        appointment dates, 168-169
    editing,
        addresses, 162-163
        appointments, 176-177
    finding
        addresses, 158-159
        appointments, 172-173
    opening
        addresses, 150-151
        appointments, 166-167

B

bars
    menu, 31
    scroll, 27-28
    title, 27, 31
booting, 17
boxes
    close, 27, 46-47
    size, 27-28
    zoom, 27-28, 52-53
by commands
by Date command (View menu), 86-87
by Kind command (View command), 90-91
by Name command (View command), 84-85
by Size command (View menu), 88-89
byte, 192

C

calculator, selecting, 144-145
Calculator commands (Apple menu), 144-145
capacity, 192
cards
    address
        adding, 154-155
        adding notes, 160-161
        deleting, 164-165
        displaying, 156-157
        editing, 162-163
        finding, 158-159
        opening, 150-151
    appointment
        adding notes, 174-175
        deleting, 178-179
        editing, 176-177
        finding, 172-173
care of the Macintosh, 28-29
changing
    alert sound, 138-139
    date, 134-135
    Desktop pattern, 130-131
    speaker volume, 132-133
    time, 136-137
characters, special, displaying, 146-147
Chooser, 192
clicking the mouse, 19, 30, 192
clipboard, 192
close, 192
close box, 27, 46-47
closing windows, 46-47
command keys, 19, 21
commands, 26-27
    by Date (View menu), 86-87

by Kind (View menu), 90-91
by Name (View menu), 84-85
by Size (View menu), 88-89
by Small Icon (View menu), 82-83
Alarm Clock (Apple menu), 140-143
Calculator (Apple menu), 144-145
Control Panel (Apple menu), 130-139
Duplicate (File menu), 100-101, 114-115
Eject (File menu), 59
Empty Trash (Special menu), 105-107
Erase Disk (Special menu), 64-65
Find Fild (Apple menu), 126-127
Get Info (File menu), 62-63, 98-99, 110-113
Key Caps (Apple menu), 146-147
New Folder (File menu), 94-95
Quit HyperCard (File menu), 152-153
Restart (Special menu), 42-43
Shut Down (Special menu), 40-41
`Completely erase disk named ___?` message, 64
computers, Macintosh, 2-5
control panel, 192
Control Panel commands (Apple menu), 130-139
copying
   disks 66-69
   documents (⌘-D key), 114-115
      to another disk, 122-123
      to another folder, 120-121
   folders (⌘-D key), 100-101
creating new folders (⌘-N key), 94-95
Ctrl key, 21

D

date, changing, 134-135
Delete key, 21
deleting
   addresses with Audio stack, 164-165
   applications, 103
   appointments with Audio stack, 178-179
   documents, 124-125
   folders (⌘-D key), 102-103
desk accessories, 4, 190-191
Desktop, 22-25, 30, 192
   changing patterns, 130-131
Desktop publishing, 183, 187-188
dialog box, 192
disk accessories, 192
disk drives, 193
disk icon, 24-25
   opening, 44-45
   renaming, 60-61
disks
   copying, 66-69
      documents into, 122-123
   displaying information, 62-63
   ejecting, 58-5
   erasing, 64-65
   floppy, 16-17, 25, 193

   formatting, 56-57
   hard, 17, 23, 25
   initializing, 56-57
   inserting, 54-55
   renaming, 60-61
displaying
   addresses with Audio stack, 156-157
   appointment dates with Audio stack, 168-169
   disk information (⌘-I key), 62-63
   document information (⌘-I), 110-111
   folder information (⌘-I key), 98-99
   special characters, 146-147
   time, 140-141
documents, 3, 30, 192
   copying, 114-115
      to another disk, 122-123
      to another folder, 120-121
   deleting, 124-125
   displaying information, 110-111
   duplicating, 114-115
   finding, 126-127
   locking, 112-113
   moving, to another folder, 118-119
   renaming, 116-117
double-clicking the mouse, 19, 30, 193
dragging the mouse, 19, 30, 193
drives
   floppy disk, 14-15, 193
   hard disk, 14-15
   inserting disks, 54-55
Duplicate command (File menu), 100-101, 114-115
duplicating documents, 114-115

E

editing
   addresses with Audio stack, 162-163
   appointments with Audio stack, 176-177
Eject command (File menu), 59
ejecting disks (⌘-E key), 58-59
ellipsis (...) following commands, 27
Empty Trash command (Special menu), 105-107
emptying trash, 106-107
enlarging windows (zoom), 52-53
Erase Disk command (Special menu), 64-65
erasing disks, 64-65

F

file, 30, 193
File menu
   Duplicate command, 100-101, 114-115
   Eject command, 59
   Get Info command, 62-63, 98-99, 110-113
   New Folder command, 94-95
   Quit HyperCard command, 152-153

files, 3, 22-23
Find File command (Apple menu), 126-127
Finder, 17, 30, 193
finding
    addresses with Audio stack, 158-159
    appointments with Audio stack, 172-173
    documents, 126-127
floppy disk drives, 14-15, 193
floppy disks, 16-17, 25, 193
    copying, 66-69
    ejecting, 58-59
    renaming, 60-61
folders, 22-23, 30, 193
    copying, 100-101
        documents into, 120-121
    creating new, 94-95
    deleting, 102-103
    displaying information, 98-99
    HyperCard, 150-179
    moving documents into, 118-119
    nesting, 95
    opening, 76-77
    renaming, 96-97
formatting disks, 56-57

G-H

Get Info command (File menu), 62-63, 98-99, 110-113

I-J

hard disk drives, 14-15
hard disks, 17, 23, 25
    renaming, 61
hardware, 14-17, 30, 193
help, 11
HyperCard, quitting, 152-153
HyperCard folder
    Addresses with Audio stack, 150-165
    Appointments with Audio stack, 166-179
icons, 22-23, 30, 193
    arranging, 74-75
    disk, 24-25
        opening, 44-45
    moving, 72-73
    Trash can, 24-25, 31, 58-59, 102-107, 125, 194
initialize, 193
initializing disks, 56-57
inserting disks, 54-55

K-L

Key Caps commands (Apple menu), 146-147
keyboard shortcuts, 22, 26
keyboards, 15, 19, 20-22

keys
    arrow, 19, 21
    command, 19, 21
    Ctrl, 21
    Delete, 21
    option, 19, 21
    Return, 21
    Shift, 21
    shortcut, 22, 26
kilobyte, 193
locking documents, 112-113

M

Macintosh, 2-5
    care of, 28-29
    desk accessories, 191
    Finder, 17
    operating system, 17-18
    restarting, 42-43
    shutting down, 40-41
    starting, 38-39
    System, 17
    turning off, 28-29, 40-41
    utilities, 191
megabyte, 193
menu bar, 24-26, 31, 193
menu commands, selecting, 26-27
menus, 193
    Apple, 126-127, 130-147
    File, 59, 62-63, 94-95, 98-99, 100-101, 110-115, 152-153
    Special, 40-43, 64-65, 105-107
    View, 82-91
messages
    Completely erase disk named ___?, 64
    Replace items with the same names with the selected items?, 119
    This disk is unreadable: Do you want to initialize it?, 56
    Two disks are different types..., 66
monitors, 14-15, 194
mouse, 15-16, 18-19
    clicking, 19
    double-clicking, 19
    dragging, 19
    pointing, 19
moving
    documents to another folder, 118-119
    icons, 72-73
    windows, 48-49

N

nesting folders, creating, 95
New Folder command (File menu), 94-95
numeric keypad, 19, 21

O

opening
    addresses with Audio stack, 150-151
    appointments with Audio stack, 166-167
    disk icons, 44-45
    folders, 76-77
option keys, 19, 21

P-Q

patterns, changing the Desktop, 130-131
pointing the mouse, 19
printer, 16
programs, 2-3, 5, 31, 194

quick reference, 182-183
Quit HyperCard command (File menu), 152-153
quitting HyperCard, 152-153

R

rearranging windows, 45
renaming
    disks, 60-61
    documents, 116-117
    folders, 96-97
Replace items with the same names with the selected items? message, 119
resizing windows, 50-51
Restart command (Special menu), 42-43
restarting the Macintosh, 42-43
retrieving items from Trash, 104-105
Return key, 21

S

scroll bars, 27-28, 194
scrolling windows, 80-81
selecting
    calculator, 144-145
    menu commands, 26-27
    windows, 78-79
setting the alarm, 142-143
Shift key, 21
shut down, 194
Shut Down command (Special menu), 40-41
shutting down the Macintosh, 40-41
size box, 27-28, 194
software, 2, 14, 17, 18, 31, 183-191, 194
speaker, changing volume, 132-133
special characters, displaying, 146-147
Special menu
    Empty Trash command, 105-107
    Erase Disk command, 64-65
    Restart command, 42-43
    Shut Down command, 40-41
starting the Macintosh, 38-39

System 7, 18
System Folder, 17, 31, 194
System software, Macintosh, 17
system unit, 14-15

T

This disk is unreadable: Do you want to initialize it? message, 56
time
    changing, 136-137
    displaying, 140-141
title bar, 27, 31, 194
Trash
    emptying, 106-107
    retrieving items from, 104-105
Trash can icon, 24-25, 31, 58-59 102-107, 125, 194
turning off the Macintosh, 28-29, 40-41
Two disks are different types... message, 66

U-V

Utilities, 190-191

View menu
    by Date command, 86-87
    by Kind command, 90-91
    by Name command, 84-85
    by Size command, 88-89
    by Small Icon command, 82-83
viewing windows
    by date, 86-87
    by icon, 82-83
    by kind, 90-91
    by name, 84-85
    by size, 88-89
volume, speaker, 132-133

W-Z

windows, 27-28, 31, 194
    closing, 46-47
    enlarging (zoom), 52-53
    moving, 48-49
    rearranging, 45
    resizing, 50-51
    scrolling, 80-81
    selecting, 78-79
    viewing, 82-91
word processors, 183-184

zoom box, 27-28, 52-53, 194